Strategy Execution and Complexity

Almost all organisations today face unprecedented levels of change, complexity and volatility. Navigating the resultant disruption dynamics is one of the most important stewardship challenges facing strategic leaders. Getting it right can pay enormous dividends, but getting it wrong can lead to spectacular failure and the ultimate demise of once admired organisations. To address this threat, strategic leaders need to better understand how to navigate complexity and volatility and how to execute strategy in this rapidly changing environment.

This book identifies 12 different strategy execution processes used to realise deliberate and emergent strategies – each illustrated with case studies and essential lessons for strategic leaders. The authors then discuss the effectiveness of these processes in different types of complex environments, showing how, used in isolation, each process can, at times, impede performance, sometimes creating survival risks that materialise today or in the future. The authors show the importance of "ambidexterity" and the need for organisations to balance the pursuit of internal efficiency and external market flexibility, both of which are essential to thriving in complex environments. This book provides essential tools for leaders to rethink and reconfigure their strategy execution practices in light of the significant change surrounding their organisations. The book is based on a 5-year, multistage study comprehensively reviewing cutting-edge research on strategy execution, reviewing seminal texts on strategy execution and, through in-depth case study interviews and cross-sectional surveys, identifying contemporary strategy execution practices of a range of different organisations across industries and sectors.

Richard Busulwa (PhD, MBA, M.Innov) is a strategy execution researcher and senior partner at Novus People, a sales and service team management advisory firm. His research focuses on strategy execution, innovation and entrepreneurship in complex environments. Richard is a member of the Strategic Management Society and the Strategy as Practice International Network.

Matthew Tice (MBA, BSc) is the chief executive officer of Insurgence, a management consulting firm dedicated to helping organisations to navigate (and lead) through disruptive change. He is a leading advisor to CEOs across the Asia-Pacific in the areas of strategy design and execution, leadership, innovation and governance. Matthew is a member of the CEO Institute (Certified) and a member of the Australian Institute of Company Directors.

Bruce Gurd (PhD, FCPA) is associate professor of management at the University of South Australia, deputy director of the Australian Centre for Asian Business and adjunct professor of Shandong University. His research is in organisational performance measures. He is a Life Fellow and recent president of the Australia and New Zealand Academy of Management (ANZAM). Bruce is also a member of the Strategic Management Society.

Strategy Execution and Complexity

Thriving in the Era of Disruption

Richard Busulwa, Matthew Tice and Bruce Gurd

Routledge
Taylor & Francis Group

LONDON AND NEW YORK

First published 2019
by Routledge
2 Park Square, Milton Park, Abingdon, Oxon OX14 4RN

and by Routledge
52 Vanderbilt Avenue, New York, NY 10017

Routledge is an imprint of the Taylor & Francis Group, an informa business

© 2019 Richard Busulwa, Matthew Tice, Bruce Gurd

The right of Richard Busulwa, Matthew Tice and Bruce Gurd to
be identified as authors of this work has been asserted by them in
accordance with sections 77 and 78 of the Copyright, Designs and
Patents Act 1988.

British Library Cataloguing-in-Publication Data
A catalogue record for this book is available from the British Library

Library of Congress Cataloging-in-Publication Data
A catalog record has been requested for this book

ISBN: 978-0-8153-7853-2 (hbk)
ISBN: 978-1-351-23219-7 (ebk)

Typeset in Bembo
by codeMantra

Contents

Figures

Part I

Types of complexity and their effects on strategy

1 Introduction and need for this book

Introduction

Our understanding of strategy execution has evolved over the last 30 years from identifying the factors for successful strategy execution to integrating these factors into cause and effect frameworks to guide strategy execution.[1,2,3] These frameworks have further evolved in recent years to become a clear set of principles and processes for executing strategy.[4,5,6,7] A number of different strategy execution processes have emerged within academic research and within practitioner books.[8] Similarly, we have made significant advances in our understanding of complexity, to the point of identifying specific types of complexity and their effects on different strategy processes.[9] In spite of these evolutions, between 60 percent and 90 percent of strategy execution efforts still fail to deliver.[10,11] We believe this is in large part due to unresolved ambiguity about the different types of strategy execution processes and their effectiveness in different contexts. Strategic leaders remain with unanswered questions such as: What are the different strategy execution processes? Do they work in practice? How are they affected by complexity? Do particular processes work better as complexity increases? Which processes will work best in my particular situation? In addition to these unanswered questions, many strategic leaders intrinsically know of processes and activities they have successfully used in practice but that aren't mentioned in mainstream research or in practitioner books. Should they abandon these as ineffective or could they actually be more effective?

Need for this book

One of the greatest challenges facing organisations today is how to improve their ability to execute strategy in the face of increasing complexity and volatility.[12,13] This complexity and volatility manifests itself as more and more unexpected events and disruptions.[14] Such unexpected events and disruptions increasingly derail strategy execution efforts – subtly at times, through initiatives that overpromise and under-deliver, and spectacularly at other times, through public failures or the demise of admired organisations.[15] Thus, there is a great and timely need to address these issues so we can move onto considering not just how organisations can adapt and survive as complexity and volatility change, but how they can thrive in complex environments.[16]

Our research has led us to believe that these issues can be addressed in five ways. First, a comprehensive review of all the strategy execution processes proposed in academic research, in practitioner books and used in practice needs to be undertaken. By doing this, we can be sure that the majority of strategy execution processes have been identified, and the key steps and activities within these processes have been unpacked and their effective use demonstrated through real-world case studies. Second, the extent to which these processes are actually used across different environments, sectors, organisation sizes and different parts of organisation value chains needs to be investigated. Third, the different types of complex environments need to be identified and the extent to which organisations actually face these types of complex environments understood. This way, we can be clear about what is theoretical complexity and what is complexity actually faced in the real world. Fourth, the effect of each type of complex environment on the different types of strategy execution processes needs to be investigated, as well as the effectiveness of each strategy process in the different types of complex environments. This way, we can know which processes work best in each type of complex environment. Finally, clarification is needed regarding the role of strategic leaders in each of the different strategy execution processes and in each type of complex environment. This way, strategic leaders can understand the roles and activities they need to perform in each strategy execution process in order to thrive in complex environments. Addressing the aforementioned issues through the five approaches, then, is the aim of this book.

Research for this book

The research for this book was undertaken in four stages. In stage one, a comprehensive review of all the academic literature on strategy execution over the last 30 years was undertaken to identify the different strategy execution processes discussed over this period. These processes were unpacked and, where necessary, synthesised into their respective steps and activities. The same process was repeated to identify the different types of complexity and to unpack their drivers.

In stage two, a comprehensive review of the leading practitioner books was undertaken to identify the different strategy execution processes and the different types of complexity discussed over this period. In order to identify the seminal books, a search for the terms "strategy", "execution", "strategy execution", "strategy implementation", "complexity" and "volatility" was undertaken on three leading online book retailing platforms (i.e. Amazon, Google Books, Apple Books). A search of the broader terminologies applying to strategy execution and complexity was also undertaken (e.g. adaptive strategy, agility, corporate longevity, strategic renewal etc.). Once a list of books was assembled, the synopsis and reader feedback of the different books was reviewed, and these were ranked for relevance and popularity. Then a search engine search for the top books for each search term was undertaken and used to modify the book rankings where there were inconsistencies. This resulted in identification of the seminal books on strategy execution and complexity, which were then reviewed in detail to identify and unpack the strategy execution processes and the types of complexity discussed.

In stage three, we went to the field to ask business leaders how they were actually executing strategy and what types of complexity they typically faced in practice. To do this, 39 interviews were conducted with senior executives, middle management and frontline employees in 13 different organisations. At these 13 organisations, an executive, middle manager and frontline employee at each organisation was interviewed for 1–3 hours. They were each asked to describe the steps involved in executing strategy at their organisation, the type of complexity faced at their organisation and by their organisation, how effective they felt their organisation was at strategy execution and what they believed needed to change to better execute strategy at their organisation as complexity changed. The responses from each organisation were only counted where two or more participants expressed that response (e.g. if an executive and frontline employee cited the same strategy execution process, then that process was deemed to be the one in use at that organisation). The interviews were recorded, transcribed and content analysed to identify strategy execution processes actually being used and types of complexity actually faced. The typical areas of frustration experienced during executing strategy as well as the improvement suggestions for these areas and for strategy execution in general were also identified.

Twelve strategy execution processes and five types of complexity were identified in the first three stages of the research. Thus, in the fourth stage, cross-sectional surveys of 241 executive, middle management and frontline employees across 83 organisations and across different organisation sizes, industries and entity types were undertaken. In the survey, participants were asked the extent to which each of the 12 strategy execution processes was in use at their organisation. They were also asked which of the strategy execution activities within each process occurred at their organisation and the extent to which these occurred. Additionally, they were asked which types of complexity were faced at their organisation, how effective they believed their organisation was at strategy execution and the extent to which particular strategy execution frustrations identified in the case study interviews applied at their organisation. The responses were analysed using both structural equation modelling and descriptive statistics.

Structure of this book

The 15 chapters of this book fall into three parts. Part I (Chapters 1–2) discusses the different types of complexity, their dynamics and how to spot each type of complexity at play. It then discusses how changes in complexity affect strategy execution in general and strategy execution processes in particular. Part II (Chapters 3–14) discusses the 12 different processes used to execute strategy. Each process has a dedicated chapter which unpacks the process' origins, the fundamental problem it seeks to solve, the process' key steps and activities, any caveats regarding use of the process, what you might know the process as, its prevalence, the types of organisations and environments it is most effective in, how you can know if your organisation is using it, its strengths and shortcomings and common tips and traps. A case study of the process in action is then provided. Each chapter also discusses the role of strategic leaders in the efficient and effective functioning of each particular process. In addition, each chapter discusses how employees can maximise their contribution to strategy execution within each process, if they are not yet a designated strategic leader. Finally, Part III discusses the ways strategic leaders can combine different processes to thrive in complex environments and the particular activities they can drive to supercharge their organisations' strategy execution efforts.

Notes

1 Miller, S. (1997). Implementing strategic decisions: Four key success factors. *Organization Science, 18*(4), 577–602.
2 Miniace, J., & Falter, E. (1996). Communication: A key factor in strategy implementation. *Strategy & Leadership, 2*(6), 26.

3 Okumus, F. (2003). A framework to implement strategies in organizations. *Management Decision, 41*(9), 871–882.
4 Busulwa, R. (2016). *The relationship between strategy execution and complexity* (PhD Thesis), University of South Australia.
5 Burgelman, R. A., & Grove, A. S. (2007). Let chaos reign, then rein in chaos – Repeatedly: Managing strategic dynamics for corporate longevity. *Strategic Management Journal, 28*(10), 964–979.
6 Davis, J., Eisenhardt, K. M., & Bingham, C. B. (2009). Optimal structure, market dynamism, and the strategy of simple rules. *Administrative Science Quarterly, 54*, 413–452.
7 Reeves, M., Love, C., & Tillmans, P. (2012). Your strategy needs a strategy. *Harvard Business Review, 90*(9), 76.
8 Busulwa, R. (2016). *The relationship between strategy execution and complexity* (PhD Thesis), University of South Australia.
9 Allen, P., Maguire, S., & McKelvey, B. (Eds.). (2011). *The sage handbook of complexity and management.* London, England: SAGE Publications.
10 Mankins, M. C., & Steele, R. (2005). Turning great strategy into great performance. *Harvard Business Review, 83*(7), 64.
11 Kaplan, R., & Norton D. (2005). The office of strategy management. *Harvard Business Review, 87*(4), 8.
12 Pascale, R. (1999). Surfing the edge of chaos. *MIT Sloan Management Review, 40*(3), 83.
13 Kotter, J. P. (2014). *Accelerate: Building strategic agility for a faster-moving world.* Boston, MA: Harvard Business School Publishing.
14 Sargut, G., & McGrath, R. (2011). Learning to live with complexity. *Harvard Business Review, 89*(9), 68.
15 Burgelman, R. A. (1991). Intraorganizational ecology of strategy making and organizational adaptation: Theory and field research. *Organization Science, 2*(3), 239–262.
16 Pascale, R. (1999). Surfing the edge of chaos. *MIT Sloan Management Review, 40*(3), 83.

2 Types of complexity and their effect on strategy processes

Strategy execution and the high failure rate

Many strategy execution approaches have been proposed over the last 30 years, but 60–90 per cent of strategy execution efforts are still reported to fail.[1,2,3] Increasing complexity and volatility is one of the top-cited causes.[4,5,6] This complexity and volatility manifests itself as more and more unexpected events and disruptions[7] that can derail strategy execution efforts. But over the last decade, advances in our understanding of complexity have turned what was once a mystery into hard science. Complexity management research has advanced to the point of identifying specific types of complexity, their dynamics and their implications for strategy execution and strategic leadership.[8,9,10]

What is complexity, really?

Complexity is one of the most overused and yet misunderstood terms in business and strategy conversations. At its heart, complexity is concerned with the underlying cause and effect behind interactions between actors, events and entities, and whether this cause and effect can be determined.[11,12] In the context of strategy, if cause and effect can be determined, then accurate predictions about the result of certain strategic actions can be made, resulting in better execution success rates.[13,14] But if it cannot be determined, then there is uncertainty about which strategic actions are necessary and which will actually work. Once strategic actions are chosen, there remains the real risk that the strategic actions chosen will turn out to be incorrect, leading to significant waste, opportunity cost, lost competitiveness and potential risk to the survival of the organisation.[15,16] The technical definition of complexity comes from complexity science, which studies the fundamental nature of complex systems. It focuses on the effect of non-linearity, or non-linear dynamics, on the behaviour of such systems. Non-linearity is the property that the magnitude of an effect or output is not linearly related to the cause or input.[17,18,19]

The effects of accurate and inaccurate predictions: the global financial crisis

The 2007 global financial crisis provides a good example of the opportunities and risks in accurate and inaccurate predictions. Most organisations did not truly or deeply understand the true cause and effect relationship behind the interactions between the actors, events, entities and subsystems of the global financial system. But, believing their understanding of the cause and effect was accurate, they proceeded to make predictions and assumptions based on the flawed belief that their business environment would be much the same as it had always been. They subsequently made strategic decisions and investment decisions based on their predictions. Their understanding of cause and effect, and thus their predictions, were grossly inaccurate. As a result, when the real cause and effect played itself out, the financial crisis came as a surprise event, and a big one at that. The resultant lack of access to new credit, clawing back of approved credit facilities, growth in payment defaults and decline in purchases dried up working capital and forced many organisations to abandon most of their strategic initiatives to free up resources for working capital. Some organisations simply could not free up the required resources in time and this led to insolvency and their eventual demise. Others were able to jettison major projects to adapt in time but incurred such significant losses that they emerged as skeletons of their former selves. Yet others thrived in the changed environment and were able to catapult themselves to new heights through acquisitions of competitors or by winning over competitors' customers. Had the cause and effect behind the interactions between the financial system's actors, entities, events and subsystems been truly known beforehand, more organisations would have been able to predict the financial crisis and many would have formed strategies to thrive during the crisis. For example, firms such as Bridgewater and Associates[20,21] and J. P. Morgan had a better understanding of the cause and effect behind the financial system and either accurately predicted the financial crisis (in the case of Bridgewater and Associates) or understood the uncertainty in predictions and had in place adaptable strategic positions (in the case of J. P. Morgan).[22]

The different types of complexity

A number of different types of complexity have been identified. These range from obvious,[23] complicated[24] and complex[25] to complex adaptive,[26] dissipative,[27] chaotic,[28] high velocity[29] and dynamic environments.[30] David Snowden, former director of knowledge management at IBM, synthesised these different types of complexity into a practitioner-oriented framework. Known as the Cynefin framework,[31] it is a tool that leaders can use to identify the type of complex environment they are faced with and therefore the approach to strategy execution that is likely to be most effective. The framework is shown in Figure 2.1, synthesizing the different types of complexity into a continuum of obvious, complicated, complex, chaotic and disorder environments. In obvious environments, the relationship between cause and effect is obvious to everyone and everyone is able to make accurate predictions.[32] In complicated environments, cause and effect is not obvious to everyone but can be discovered through analysis or through the use of experts. Thus, accurate predictions can be made on the basis of analysis or relevant expertise. In complex environments, cause and effect can be determined but only in retrospect, making accurate prediction difficult. In chaotic environments, there is no relationship between cause and effect; cause and effect cannot be discovered prospectively or retrospectively, and accurate predictions cannot be made. Finally, in disorder environments, multiple types of complexity jostle for prominence with cacophony ruling.

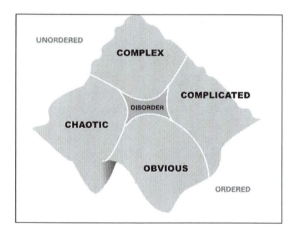

Figure 2.1 The Cynefin framework and its different types of complexity[33]

To determine the type of complexity faced, the framework calls on practitioners' collective judgements about the nature of the cause and effect they face and the ease with which accurate predictions can be made.[34] For example, if they find it is difficult to determine cause and effect in advance, find it difficult to accurately predict what will happen in the future, and find that the causes of events can only be determined in retrospect, then they can make the judgement that they operate in a complex environment. Knowing they are operating in a complex environment, they can then use the strategy processes that optimise strategy realisation in complex environments.

Unfortunately, some organisations face changing types of complexity or multiple types of complexity simultaneously.[35] Volatility, in contrast to complexity, is concerned with the speed of change from one type of complexity to another and the diversity in the types of complexity being changed to.[36] For example, a military organisation may shift between obvious and chaotic environments but do this very infrequently. In contrast, a high technology firm may shift from an obvious to a chaotic to a complex environment within weeks or months. In this case, the technology firm has a higher rate of volatility, as the speed of change in type of complexity is higher and the diversity in the types of complexity changed to is greater. High technology firm environments are sometimes also referred to as high velocity[37] environments because of their reputation for extraordinary complexity, rapid and diverse changes and fleeting windows of opportunity.

Effects of complexity on strategy processes

Complexity affects strategy execution in three fundamental ways. First, it affects the degree to which predictions about the future can be relied upon and used as a basis on which to form strategies.[38] In obvious and complicated environments, the cause and effect can be discovered in advance and used to make accurate predictions.[39] These predictions can then be used as the basis for forming deliberate strategies. This is consistent with much of the classical strategy literature which prescribes analysing the anticipated future business environment, identifying an optimal strategic position in that future business environment and executing to realise that strategic position.[40] But in complex and chaotic environments, cause and effect is often not discoverable in advance. As a result, making accurate predictions is difficult and investing in initiatives based on predictions in such an environment can be outright dangerous. For example, consider the firms that explicitly or implicitly predicted a continuation of the status quo business environment for 2007 (e.g. continued availability of easy credit plus continued growth in real estate prices). Many of these firms put capital at risk via strategic initiatives based on these predictions. They subsequently found themselves in a dangerous situation relative to firms that formed more flexible strategies, on the basis that anything could happen or knowing that the financial crisis was coming. The more difficult it is to make accurate predictions about the future, the more effective strategy processes that encourage a test and adapt, improvisation and self-organised response to changing conditions are.[41,42,43] In contrast, when it is possible to make accurate predictions about the future, such strategy execution processes may be wasteful and those that constrain the autonomous actions of employees to focus on the efficient realisation of deliberate strategies are more effective.[44]

Second, complexity influences whether deliberate strategy, emergent strategy or a mixture of both will be realised.[45] Deliberate strategies are largely dependent on making accurate predictions. As a result, deliberate strategies are difficult to form with confidence and rarely work out in complex and chaotic environments. For example, a strategic initiative to build a big dam in March based on predictions of perfect weather is unlikely to work out if, midway through March, severe floods and storms eventuate. The more complex environments are, the more these environments impede the success rate of deliberate strategies and improve the success rate of emergent strategies. When the type of complex environment faced is constantly changing between environments in which predictions can be made and environments in which predictions cannot be made, hedging with a combination of deliberate and emergent strategies results in better strategy execution effectiveness.[46,47] That is, in such situations, strategic leaders should ensure organisations use the adequate mix of strategy execution processes that drive the realisation of emergent strategies as well as strategy execution processes that drive the delivery of deliberate strategies.

Finally, complexity influences the perceptions of employees and, as a result, their engagement levels[48] and resistance to or motivation towards strategy execution efforts.[49] Like strategic leaders, employees form their own cause and effect logic about events occurring within and outside of their organisation. They then make predictions about their future and the future of their organisations. These predictions and the cause and effect behind them influence employees' engagement levels and resultant decisions. For example, employees who perceive that their organisation needs to embrace emerging technologies in order to better serve customers and stay ahead of the competition are likely to become frustrated if their organisation introduces strategies that don't address this need. This may lead them to decide to move to an organisation that embraces emerging technologies. The challenge is, as complexity increases, an employee's cause and effect and predictions become less and less accurate.[50] But although uncertain and often incorrect, these logics and predictions may negatively influence engagement levels. In the absence of strategic leadership interventions, such negative influences on engagement can stifle both anticipated strategy execution effectiveness and actual strategy execution effectiveness. In Figure 2.2, we show the commonly perceived strategy execution frustration areas cited by executive, middle management and frontline employee participants in our study.[51] Depending on the type of complexity faced, organisations may need to pay particular attention to the areas described.

Frustration Area or Area Needing Improvement	Executive	Frontline Management/ middle management	Front Line Employees
Degree of Strategy Consultation/Bottom Up Input	33%	30%	37%
Speed of Resource Redeployment	38%	30%	32%
Speed of Strategy Refresh	39%	25%	36%
Level of Engagement Building	39%	29%	33%
Effectiveness of Strategy Communication	38%	32%	30%
Effectiveness of Purpose Building	38%	30%	32%
Level of Autonomy	28%	30%	42%
Genuine and Realisable Incentives (Real Incentives)	36%	26%	38%
Aligned Incentives & Disincentives	36%	24%	39%
Strategy Justification/Rationale	35%	31%	34%
Leadership Capability at lower levels	30%	30%	40%
Effective Alignment of Power Brokers	31%	29%	40%
Sufficient Implementation Resourcing	37%	26%	37%
Effective Supporting IT Infrastructure	38%	28%	33%

Figure 2.2 Areas cited by employees as needing improvement and proportion of respondents within each group citing them.[52]

Note: This table shows respondents citing that issue as a proportion of the total respondents in that group. For example, 33 per cent of the executive team members that participated in our study cited strategy consultation as a frustration area or area needing improvement. This table differs to the one shown in Busulwa (2016) which depicts percentage responses as a proportion of total study participants.

What can be done about the effects of complexity on strategy processes?

We see four key things that strategic leaders can do to manage the effects of complexity. First, they need to get a clear understanding of the different types of complexity and cultivate the ability to diagnose the types of complexity that are at play. By knowing the type of complex environment their organisation or parts of their organisation face, strategic leaders will be better positioned to understand how that type of complexity will affect the strategy processes they use, how it will affect the type of strategy being pursued and how it will affect the perceptions of employees and other stakeholders.[53] Being able to diagnose the type of complexity at play also enables strategic leaders to spot when the type of complexity at play is changing. Second, strategic leaders can ensure that their organisations pursue the right types of strategies for their environment. For instance, organisations in complex and chaotic environments ought to pursue emergent strategies; notwithstanding that they can also pursue deliberate strategies in parallel for more predictable sub-environments. If organisations in complex environments only pursue deliberate strategies, it is likely that their competitiveness and, perhaps, long-term survival will be compromised. Having identified the types of strategies to pursue, strategic leaders then need to ensure their organisations use the most effective strategy execution processes to realise those types of strategies. For example, using a process like the Execution Premium (outlined in Chapter 4) to pursue emergent strategies is likely to constrain the organisation's ability to realise these emergent strategies. But using another process, such as the Resource Allocation process (outline in Chapter 9), would minimise constraints on the realisation of emergent strategy. Finally, strategic leaders can play an active role in limiting the negative effects of complexity on employee and stakeholder perceptions of the organisation's actions (or non-actions) and thus their engagement levels. By maintaining constructive perceptions and high engagement levels, strategic leaders can accelerate strategy execution efforts rather than let complexity derail them.

Notes

1 Kaplan, R., & Norton, D. (2005). The office of strategy management. *Harvard Business Review, 87*(4), 8.
2 Miller, D. (2002). Successful change leaders: What makes them? What do they do that is different? *Journal of Change Management, 2*(4), 359.
3 Mankins, M. C., & Steele, R. (2005). Turning great strategy into great performance. *Harvard Business Review, 83*(7), 64.

4   Pascale, R. T. (1999). Surfing the edge of chaos. *Sloan Management Review, 40*(3), 83.

5   Pascale, R. (1999). Surfing the edge of chaos. *MIT Sloan Management Review, 40*(3), 83.

6   Burgelman, R. A., & Grove, A. S. (2007). Let chaos reign, then rein in chaos – repeatedly: Managing strategic dynamics for corporate longevity. *Strategic Management Journal, 28*(10), 964–979.

7   Sargut, G., & McGrath, R. G. (2011). Learning to live with complexity. *Harvard Business Review, 89*(9), 68–76.

8   Burgelman, R. A., & Grove, A. S. (2007). Let chaos reign, then rein in chaos – repeatedly: Managing strategic dynamics for corporate longevity. *Strategic Management Journal, 28*(10), 964–979.

9   Davis, J., Eisenhardt, K. M., & Bingham, C. B. (2009). Optimal structure, market dynamism, and the strategy of simple rules. *Administrative Science Quarterly, 54*, 413–452.

10 Snowden, D. J., & Boone, M. (2007). A leader's framework for decision making. *Harvard Business Review, 85*(11), 68.

11 Sargut, G., & McGrath, R. (2011). Learning to live with complexity. *Harvard Business Review, 89*(9), 68.

12 Snowden, D. J., & Boone, M. (2007). A leader's framework for decision making. *Harvard Business Review, 85*(11), 68.

13 Sargut, G., & McGrath, R. (2011). Learning to live with complexity. *Harvard Business Review, 89*(9), 68.

14 Snowden, D. J., & Boone, M. (2007) A leader's framework for decision making. *Harvard Business Review, 85*(11), 68.

15 Sargut, G., & McGrath, R. (2011). Learning to live with complexity. *Harvard Business Review, 89*(9), 68.

16 Snowden, D. J., & Boone, M. (2007). A leader's framework for decision making. *Harvard Business Review, 85*(11), 68.

17 Nicolis, G., & Prigogine, I. (1989). Exploring complexity: An introduction. New York, NY: W. H. Freeman.

18 Burgelman, R. A., & Grove, A. S. (2007). Let chaos reign, then rein in chaos – repeatedly: Managing strategic dynamics for corporate longevity. *Strategic Management Journal, 28*(10), 964–979.

19 Pascale, R. (1999). Surfing the edge of chaos. *MIT Sloan Management Review, 40*(3), 83.

20 Cassidy, J. (2011). "Mastering the machine: how Ray Dalio built the world's richest and strangest hedge fund". *The New Yorker, 25 July*, 56–65.

21 Dalio, R. (2017). *Principles: Life and work.* New York, NY: Simon and Schuster.

22 Sorkin, A. R. (2008). JP Morgan raises bid for bear stearns to $10 a share. *The New York Times,* 17.

23 Snowden, D. J., & Boone, M. (2007). A leader's framework for decision making. *Harvard Business Review, 85*(11), 68.

24 Snowden, D. J., & Boone, M. (2007). A leader's framework for decision making. *Harvard Business Review, 85*(11), 68.

25 Burgelman, R. A., & Grove, A. S. (2007). Let chaos reign, then rein in chaos – repeatedly: Managing strategic dynamics for corporate longevity. *Strategic Management Journal, 28*(10), 964–979.

26 Holland, J. H. (2006). Studying complex adaptive systems. *Journal of Systems Science and Complexity, 19*(1), 1–8.

27 Leifer, R. (1989). Understanding organization transformation using a dissipative structure model. *Human Relations, 42*(10), 899–916.
28 Snowden, D. J., & Boone, M. (2007). A leader's framework for decision making. *Harvard Business Review, 85*(11), 68.
29 Davis, J., Eisenhardt, K. M., & Bingham, C. B. (2009). Optimal structure, market dynamism, and the strategy of simple rules. *Administrative Science Quarterly, 54*, 413–452.
30 Davis, J., Eisenhardt, K. M., & Bingham, C. B. (2009). Optimal structure, market dynamism, and the strategy of simple rules. *Administrative Science Quarterly, 54*, 413–452.
31 Snowden, D. J., & Boone, M. (2007). A leader's framework for decision making. *Harvard Business Review, 85*(11), 68.
32 Snowden, D. J., & Boone, M. (2007). A leader's framework for decision making. *Harvard Business Review, 85*(11), 68.
33 Snowden, D. J., & Boone, M. (2007). A leader's framework for decision making. *Harvard Business Review, 85*(11), 68.
34 Snowden, D. J., & Boone, M. (2007). A leader's framework for decision making. *Harvard Business Review, 85*(11), 68.
35 Burgelman, R. A., & Grove, A. S. (2007). Let chaos reign, then rein in chaos – repeatedly: Managing strategic dynamics for corporate longevity. *Strategic Management Journal, 28*(10), 964–979.
36 Davis, J., Eisenhardt, K. M., & Bingham, C. B. (2009). Optimal structure, market dynamism, and the strategy of simple rules. *Administrative Science Quarterly, 54*, 413–452.
37 Davis, J., Eisenhardt, K. M., & Bingham, C. B. (2009). Optimal structure, market dynamism, and the strategy of simple rules. *Administrative Science Quarterly, 54*, 413–452.
38 Sargut, G., & McGrath, R. (2011). Learning to live with complexity. *Harvard Business Review, 89*(9), 68.
39 Snowden, D. J., & Boone, M. (2007). A leader's framework for decision making. Harvard Business Review, *85*(11), 68.
40 Porter, M. E. (1996, November/December). What is strategy. *Harvard Business Review.*
41 Davis, J., Eisenhardt, K. M., & Bingham, C. B. (2009). Optimal structure, market dynamism, and the strategy of simple rules. *Administrative Science Quarterly, 54*, 413–452.
42 Burgelman, R. A., & Grove, A. S. (2007). Let chaos reign, then rein in chaos – repeatedly: Managing strategic dynamics for corporate longevity. *Strategic Management Journal, 28*(10), 964–979.
43 Eisenhardt, K., & Brown, S. (1998). Competing on the edge: Strategy as structured chaos. *Long Range Planning, 31*(5), 786–789.
44 Raisch, S., Birkinshaw, J., Probst, G., & Tushman, M. L. (2009). Organizational ambidexterity: Balancing exploitation and exploration for sustained performance. *Organization Science, 20*, 685–695.
45 Nielsen, B. B. (2009). Adaptive strategy making: The effects of emergent and intended strategy modes. *European Management Review, 6*(2), 94–106.
46 Burgelman, R. A., & Grove, A. S. (2007). Let chaos reign, then rein in chaos – repeatedly: Managing strategic dynamics for corporate longevity. *Strategic Management Journal, 28*(10), 964–979.

47 Markides, C., & Chu, W. (2009). Innovation through Ambidexterity: How to achieve the ambidextrous organization. *Handbook of Research on Strategy and Foresight, 324.*

48 Busulwa, R. (2016). *The relationship between strategy execution and complexity* (Ph.D. Thesis), University of South Australia.

49 Busulwa, R. (2016). *The relationship between strategy execution and complexity* (Ph.D. Thesis), University of South Australia.

50 Busulwa, R. (2016). *The relationship between strategy execution and complexity* (Ph.D. Thesis), University of South Australia.

51 Busulwa, R (2016). *The relationship between strategy execution and complexity* (Ph.D. Thesis), University of South Australia.

52 Busulwa, R. (2016). *The relationship between strategy execution and complexity* (Ph.D. Thesis), University of South Australia.

53 Burgelman, R. A., & Grove, A. S. (2007). Let chaos reign, then rein in chaos – repeatedly: Managing strategic dynamics for corporate longevity. *Strategic Management Journal, 28*(10), 964–979.

Part II

Types of strategy execution processes

3   The 7 Factor Process

Origin and design principles

Origin

The 7 Factor Process is one of the processes drawn from academic research on strategy execution. The research was originally undertaken by Fevzi Okumus, a professor of strategic management at the University of Central Florida. In early 2000, he undertook a comprehensive review and categorisation of all the research on strategy implementation in existence at that time.[1] He found that most of the existing research had focused on identifying the factors for successful strategy implementation. But he also noticed that there was a seemingly endless number of factors for success.[1] Further, there was little discussion of the interrelationships between the different factors identified. Teasing out the definitions of the different factors, the overlaps, the duplications and slippery terms, Okumus was able to synthesise the existing body of work into 11 factors. Further teasing out the interrelationships between the factors, he then translated these 11 factors into a strategy execution framework.[1] For the purpose of this book, we were only interested in the overall process and the activities or activity groups within the process. We identified seven such activities or activity groups and synthesised these into "The 7 Factor Process" to reflect Fevzi Okumus' research focused on factors.

The problem

As Fevzi Okumus noted,[1] prior to his study there had been little focus on how different factors interacted with each other and the resultant impact of these interactions on strategy execution. To be clear, there had been a number of research-based strategy implementation frameworks proposed since the 1980s. But an inherent challenge in the reliability of these frameworks lay in the many different factors identified, the inconsistent language used and the ambiguity over whether they were addressing strategy content, strategy process or strategy outcomes. Also, until Okumus' research, there had been little discussion on how the different factors interacted with an organisation's internal and external environment and the resultant effect of this on strategy execution. The research underpinning the 7 Factor Process addressed three long-standing strategy execution issues. First, it identified the essential strategy execution factors and thus limited the further proliferation of factors. Second, it shifted the research and practice conversation from a discussion of factors and practices for successful strategy execution to a discussion of strategy execution activities or groups of activities. And third, it emphasised the importance of exploring how the different strategy execution activities interacted with each other and with the changing internal and external environment to affect strategy execution effectiveness.

The idea in brief

The 7 Factor Process identifies seven factors or activity areas that are essential to effective strategy execution. These activity areas are as follows: (1) form the strategy, (2) prepare, plan and pilot implementation activities, (3) allocate financial, time and talent resources for strategy execution, (4) communicate and sell the strategy, (5) recruit, train, incentivise and develop competencies for strategy implementation, (6) formally and informally monitor and compare the efforts and results of the implementation with predetermined outcomes and (7) learn from intended and unintended outcomes of the process (see Figure 3.1).

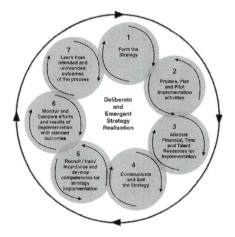

Figure 3.1 The 7 Factor Process.

Factor 1: Form the strategy is concerned with the continuous monitoring and evaluation of the organisation's external and internal environment to identify threats and opportunities and, subsequently, to form executable strategies to capitalise on the opportunities and mitigate the threats. While there is a lot written about how to undertake external environment analysis and what tools to use, Okumus warns that spending adequate time on internal environment issues is equally important. In particular, he identified five key internal environment issues or questions for strategic leaders to consider and plan for:

1. How is the new strategy likely to change job roles and duties, decision-making processes and decision rights and reporting relationships? What is the likely impact of these changes on the organisation's ability to execute the strategy?
2. Does the current or proposed organisation structure have the ability to facilitate the sufficient free flow of information, coordination of workflows and cooperation between different management levels and functional areas to enable realisation of the strategy?
3. What is the likely impact of the new strategy on informal networks, politics and key stakeholders, and how will this impact in turn affect strategy execution?
4. What is the likely attitude of powerful groups in the organisation to the new strategy, and how will this attitude affect execution of the strategy?
5. What is the likely impact of the new strategy on the organisation's existing culture and subcultures, and what are the implications for executing the new strategy?

Factor 2: Prepare, plan and pilot implementation activities is concerned with translating the strategy into operational initiatives, projects and tasks. Fevzi Okumus advises that strategic leaders should ensure this step is undertaken with participation and feedback from different management and functional areas and that intended initiatives or projects are trialled to provide the opportunity to learn about the opportunities and risks before large-scale implementation.

Factor 3: Allocate financial, time and talent resources for strategy execution is aimed at making sure that there are adequate financial, time and talent resources dedicated to implementing strategy. Perceptions of which resources are needed and what consists "adequate" levels of each resource may differ across different organisation stakeholders. Nevertheless, all stakeholders would agree that there are levels of resourcing that may inadvertently set particular initiatives or projects up for failure. Fevzi Okumus cautions that strategic leaders should consider how the procedure for securing resources, as well as the cultural and political issues related to resource allocation, will impact strategy implementation.

Factor 4: communicate and sell the strategy aims to effectively communicate the strategy and to justify the strategy to the organisation's stakeholders. Okumus advises that strategic leaders should consider bringing to bear the most effective modes of communication for their particular environment. For example, communication may be top-down or bottom-up, formal or informal, internal or external, one-time or in continuous mode, lateral or not lateral, digital or face-to-face. Similarly, the most effective modes of communication should be used that take into account the unique communication challenges of each organisation. For example, in some organisations, communication channels such as meetings, emails and newsletters may be effective, while in others, channels such as town hall forums, website posters and signs on the back of toilet doors and offsite sessions may be effective (e.g. you can do an online search for the Cricket Australia strategy to see Cricket Australia's approach to communicating its strategy online). Given differences in individual learning preferences, a mixture of communication channels may be helpful to maximise understanding and buy-in.

Factor 5: recruit, train, incentivise and develop competencies for strategy implementation aims to ensure that people with the right competencies for effective strategy execution are in place, that these competencies are continuously upgraded and that these people have the right incentives and disincentives for the efficient and effective execution of strategy. For example, if strategic leaders wished the strategy of a sales organisation to emphasise sales growth in a particular industry, they may want to have the best sales leaders and trainers on that team; they may want to provide them with the best incentives (e.g. performance bonuses); and they may want to ensure the best opportunities for growth and development are provided.

Factor 6: formally and informally monitor and compare the efforts and results of the implementation with predetermined outcomes is concerned with monitoring the efficiency and effectiveness of strategy execution efforts. Internal and external environments are subject to constant change and to surprising events that can derail strategy execution efforts or the effect of predetermined outcomes.

Where efforts and outcomes are inconsistent with expectations, this factor ensures that strategic leaders have the opportunity to understand this in as close to real time as possible. Armed with this information, they have the opportunity to modify efforts or expectations as necessary.

Factor 7: learn from intended and unintended outcomes of the process aims to ensure that strategic leaders and their organisations learn from what works and what doesn't work. In complicated, complex and changing environments, unintended consequences can result from strategy execution efforts and outcomes. Factor 7 proposes that strategic leaders put in place the best approaches to ensure ongoing learning and necessary future adjustments to the strategy are made so they can be more effective over time.

Caveats

There are some important caveats related to this process. The first is that it does not suggest or imply that strategy execution is neat, linear and sequential, nor that strategy formation and implementation are different and separate phases of strategy realisation. Rather, the key activities identified should be taken as iterative processes that happen in organisations every day. For example, Factor 4, "Communicate and sell the strategy", is the daily task of leaders who wish to ensure their employees understand the direction the organisation is going, the reason for that direction, as well as why and how they should contribute to it.

What you might know it as

If you are familiar with the Execution Premium Process by Robert Kaplan and David Norton, the 7 Factor Process is very similar, albeit with less prescription regarding how to carry out activities and the tools to use in carrying out each activity. When the Execution Premium Process was introduced in 2008, it provided far more formal structures and tools to use for each factor within the 7 Factor Process. It was also written for a managerial audience, whereas the 7 Factor Process was more aimed at a research audience. Given these issues and given that the Execution Premium Process came out shortly after academic publication of the 7 Factor Process, it is likely you may not know of it by name but understand the factors.

Prevalence

Across all sectors, we found 13 per cent of organisations, or one in every ten organisations, to be using the 7 Factor Process to execute strategy. Although the process was used across all sectors, it was most commonly used in the non-governmental organisation/not-for-profit (NGO/NFP) sectors, where more than one in every four organisations cited its use. In contrast, one in ten organisations within the private sector and the public sector used the process. More than half of the organisations making extensive use of this process (53%) cited high to very high strategy execution effectiveness. Across organisation sizes, the process was most used by organisations with more than 500 employees. Such organisations used this process twice as much as organisations with less than 500 employees. Across all sectors and organisation sizes, the 7 Factor Process was generally used less often than other formal processes. A part of the cause for this may be due to practitioners not being familiar with the process name, perhaps due to its origins in academic research. This was particularly apparent in the case study interviews. In these interviews, we asked participants if they used the 7 Factor Process, and many responded that they did not. But when we later asked them to describe the key activities carried out to execute strategy at their organisation, they described many of the steps in the 7 Factor Process, implying at least an implicit understanding of the process (Figure 3.2).

| Process | Sector | | | | Employees (Org Size) | | | | |
	Public Sector / Government	Private Sector	NGO/NFP	All Sectors	>500	51-499	2 - 50	<2	All Sizes
7 Factor Process	10%	13%	25%	13%	19%	10%	10%	0%	12%
Execution Premium Process	24%	16%	25%	18%	25%	21%	13%	11%	18%
Simple Rules	14%	20%	17%	18%	13%	21%	23%	44%	21%
Lean Strategy Deployment Process	14%	19%	25%	18%	22%	21%	15%	11%	18%
Change Acceleration Process	14%	11%	17%	12%	9%	21%	10%	11%	12%
Project Management Process	53%	80%	66%	70%	88%	84%	63%	33%	72%
Talent Placement Process	14%	27%	25%	23%	22%	26%	23%	11%	22%
Outcomes and Incentives / Disincentives Communication Process	24%	28%	25%	26%	31%	26%	25%	11%	26%
Learning on the Run Process	39%	38%	50%	38%	31%	42%	43%	22%	37%
Resource Allocation / Portfolio Management Process	19%	17%	25%	18%	22%	21%	18%	66%	24%
Performance Monitoring and Feedback Process	39%	38%	50%	38%	44%	37%	43%	0%	38%

Figure 3.2 Proportion of study participants citing use of the 7 Factor Process by sector and organisation size.

Note: *For example, of the 241 study participants, 50 participants were from the public sector/government. Of these 50 public sector/government participants, 5 participants (10%) used the 7 Factor Process. This table differs from Tables 6.23 and 6.24 shown in Busulwa (2016)[6], where process users in each sector are shown as a proportion of all study participants.

The process in action

Each of the 7 factors or activity groups is meant to be carried out continuously. For example, Factor 4, "Communicate and sell the strategy", is the daily task of leaders wanting to ensure that at all times the people on their team understand where the organisation is going, why it is going there and what they can do to best support it to get there. But the 7 factors are also meant to operate as an iterative process happening in organisations every day. The 7 Factor Process leaves users with a lot of discretion as to how each activity is carried out and what tools are used to carry it out. For instance, we noted earlier how Factor 4 can be carried out by a strategic leader choosing the communication mode (e.g. top-down or bottom-up, formal or informal, internal or external, one-time or in continuous mode, lateral or not lateral, digital or face-to-face) that best suits their style and their unique context as well as by choosing a channel (e.g. company-wide forums, review meetings, emails, middle and frontline managers, newsletters, posters etc.) that best suits their style and context. By applying Factors 6 and 7 well, strategic leaders can learn over time what works best for their unique styles and contexts for each factor. What follows next is a case study demonstrating the process in action. We have used the case study of an emergency department in a large public teaching hospital in Australia. As you read the case, pay attention to the approach taken by the emergency department for each factor. This is the approach that suited the unique situation of the emergency department. If the 7 Factor Process suits your unique situation, you may be able to come up with a better approach to achieving the objectives of each factor.

Case study: redeveloping the Flinders Medical Centre Emergency Department

Flinders Medical Centre is a large 593-bed public teaching hospital in Australia. It is part of a hospital and healthcare network which is funded by the state Department of Health. Earlier reviews of the internal and external environment of the statewide health system[2] had revealed growing attendances at the hospital's emergency department, ageing building infrastructure that limited capacity of the emergency department and thus a need to redesign/redevelop the emergency department to meet future demands.[3] Hospital senior management decided to pursue the redesign and redevelopment strategic initiative in 2009 after receiving endorsement from the Department of Health.

Senior management facilitated the preparation of draft plans and implementation activities and consulted with clinical and non-clinical management teams within the emergency department, within the broader hospital and within the broader hospital network of stakeholders. After a lot of feedback and several iterations of the draft plans, the implementation plans were finally agreed on by clinical leaders and signed off by the executive team. Pilot projects and activities were incorporated into the implementation plans. As pilot projects were implemented, a range of unanticipated issues emerged. For example, a pilot hospital avoidance strategy project expected to temporarily reduce emergency department attendances during the rebuild resulted in less attendances to the emergency department but an increase in complex attendances, which took more time to treat and thus increased department workload. Other unanticipated issues, largely related to workflows and patient experience impacts, were not previously visible to senior management and thus not considered during initial planning phase. These and other lessons learned from the pilot implementation initiatives and activities were regularly reviewed and used to further refine and modify the remaining implementation plans. For example, capacity was temporarily upgraded at nearby hospitals in the network to supplement the hospital avoidance projects following the results from the trial of these projects.

Senior management received funding and thus a separate budget to carry out the redevelopment strategic initiative. This enabled the allocation of dedicated time and talent resources to carry out the implementation activities. For example, there were specialist project managers, clinical change leaders and process redesign experts funded to work on the project within the emergency department, within the broader hospital and at the executive level.

Given that hospitals are complex by nature and the emergency department operated over 24 hours, communication was a big challenge for initiative leads who only worked during the day. As a result, almost all conceivable modes of communication were undertaken, including top-down, bottom-up, lateral, formal, informal, internal, external, one-time and continuous modes. For instance, weekly progress reviews and debriefing sessions were set up across different clinical groups and across shifts to update stakeholders on progress, lessons learned and anticipated issues, as well as to capture ongoing feedback. These groups included the medical hierarchy across all shifts over the 24 hours of operation, the nursing hierarchy across all shifts, the patient services hierarchy across all shifts, security teams, scientific teams, support service teams and many others. Key stakeholder communication meetings were organised with external stakeholders such as ministerial advisers, unions, professional bodies and accreditation agencies. External communication was undertaken with the community via the corporate communications unit to prepare prospective department attendees for the changed patient experience and to limit potential distracting media attention or politicisation of changes. The staff and patient benefits of the new department were emphasised to keep staff engaged in the change.

Medical, nursing and clinical support staff roles changed as workflows changed with the department layout. For example, geographic separation of groups of care activities related to the new department design meant an expansion of supervision activities for roles with previously limited supervision scope and experience. Ultimately, the organisational structure of the department was modified to accommodate the change in workflows and in decision-making requirements. This then led to some hospital-wide change in roles. For example, a role was created at the executive level for escalation of political/legal risk issues that emerged due to the redevelopment. Early and ongoing consultation and communication with powerful groups and subgroups within the organisation were essential to the changes in roles being able to occur with minimal risk.

Project management, change management, clinical process redesign and other competencies relevant to the project were recruited; in some cases, these competencies were trained for through regular workshops and in-house coaches, as the competencies were required in combination with clinical competencies. Staff change incentives were planned that included career development opportunities for change leaders and formal and informal celebration of achievements. Formal and informal monitoring of implementation activities and outcomes occurred through regular progress review meetings, daily analysis of demand, capacity and efficiency KPIs and site visits. Lessons learned from intended and unintended outcomes were incorporated into plans that were still to be implemented.

The department redevelopment was successfully completed in late 2011.[4] Attendance at the department increased significantly as soon as it was completed and soon exceeded the expanded department capacity. As large, extensive and time consuming as the consultation on implementation plans had been, it did not anticipate that attendances would almost immediately exceed department capacity as soon as the department was completed. As a result, the broader state healthcare system was unprepared for what ambulances would do with patients if they arrived while the department was full and what the resultant flow on effects of this would be. This in turn resulted in "ramping" or queuing of ambulances outside of the department until free patient spaces could become available. This restricted the ability of ambulances to then respond to subsequent jobs. This in turn caused unfavourable media attention and disputes between ambulance services union, emergency department staff and medical and nursing unions, as well as department of health management over the true causes of the issue and resultant duty of care risks.[5] This highlights the critical importance of Factors 2 and 4 in this process and that strategic leaders should not be afraid to overdo piloting and internal and external consultation and communication, as under-doing these can tarnish otherwise great execution.

Are you in the right environment for this process?

The 7 Factor Process requires strong strategic leadership to drive it as well as a lot of day-to-day involvement in all factors by strategic leaders. This is due to the fact that it provides so much discretion as to how each factor can be carried out. Thus, if strategic leaders do not exercise their discretion and creativity to make choices regarding actions to be carried out within that factor, or at least delegate it, nothing may be happening within that factor. Alternatively, strategy derailing actions (e.g. misleading or self-serving communication) may fill the action void. In either case, the lack of strategic leadership within that factor may compromise the realisation of intended strategies. In our research, we found the process to be most effective where span of control is not so large, the number of hierarchical levels isn't too problematic, the organisation isn't so complicated and the environment isn't so complex or volatile. This is in contrast to environments that are of such high velocity, volatility or complexity that deliberate strategies cannot be pursued. If applied in an environment not well suited to it (e.g. a high velocity or chaotic environment), the 7 Factor Process is likely to result in a significant number of failed strategic initiatives and thus misallocated or wasted resources that may eventually threaten the ability of the organisation to compete successfully in the long run.

Knowing when you are using it

Many organisations can use one or more strategy execution processes without being aware of their use. For example, in our study, we found that at the same organisation executives may cite one process being in use at their organisation, while middle managers cited another and frontline and functional employees cite an altogether different one. And in multi-business or multi-geography firms, different business units or geographic areas might use different processes. The telltale signs that this process is in use are usually visible in Factors 2–6. If this process is being used effectively, you should see strategic initiatives being piloted prior to implementation, you should see senior leaders actively involved in the allocation of resources to these strategic initiatives, you should see regular communication and justification of the strategy so that everyone at your organisation understands what the strategy is and what their role in it is. You should also see discussions of how recruitment, incentives and competencies will be configured to support the achievement of strategic priorities and initiatives.

Process strengths and shortcomings

A key strength of the 7 Factor Process is that it identifies the essential action areas, objectives and desired outcomes, but leaves managers the discretion to decide the specific actions they take and the methods or tools they use in carrying out those actions. In doing so, it provides them with the opportunity to tailor the process to their unique leadership styles and experiences as well as their organisation's unique circumstances. A potential shortcoming of the process is that it has a heavy bias towards the pursuit of deliberate strategies. That is, it does not explicitly address the encouragement and pursuit of emergent strategies, which are essential for adapting to changing environments.[2]

Common tips and traps

A common trap with any process is to see it and attempt to use it as sequential process, with each factor awaiting the full completion of the prior factor before beginning. This is as opposed to seeing each factor and all factors collectively operating as ongoing iterative processes of prototyping, testing, modification and retesting until strategy is realised.[3] In both approaches, the strategy may be undermined by issues such as complexity, dynamism and surprising events that might make it irrelevant as soon as it is made.[4] However, whereas the latter approach enables timely issue identification and course correction, the former is much less amenable to this. Subsequently, it is more likely to result in the ongoing pursuit of strategies that are irrelevant or have much longer strategy refresh delays. Another common trap with the 7 Factor Process is insufficient executive leadership and involvement within the different factors. Because the process leaves a lot of discretion to customise the approach to each factor to the organisation's unique circumstances, lack of executive involvement may mean that firms don't identify and explicitly pursue actions within each factor that are best suited to their unique setting. For example, in the emergency department case study described earlier, lack of senior management team involvement in any of the factors would have undermined the potential success of the project given the interrelatedness of all the factors. While top management team involvement is essential for all processes, it is particularly essential in this process. Where the top management team simply does not have the time required to lead and be involved in all the factors, this may not be the best process to use. Alternatively, if it is still to be used, strategic leaders should limit the number of strategic initiatives on the go to a level that allows for their necessary involvement and leadership of each factor.

Spotlight on the role of strategic leaders

Strategic leaders are the people on the top management team or the dominant coalition within the organisation. Their most important role is to ensure the realisation of strategies that balance the efficient pursuit of today's threats and opportunities with building capacity to adapt to tomorrow's threats and opportunities. This is often referred to as achieving the optimal balance between the efficiency and adaptation or efficiency and flexibility. A large part of achieving the efficiency challenge is discharged through maximisation of the efficiency and effectiveness with which the activities within each factor are carried out. Whilst strategic leaders can delegate particular factors or activities, they are accountable for the ultimate success or failure of these factors and activities and of the overall process. Some strategic leaders fail to discharge their duties by focusing too much on one factor at the expense of others – all factors are essential. Other strategic leaders fail to discharge their duties by delegating particular factors or activities in such a manner that it is essentially abdication.

What if you are not a strategic leader?

This particular strategy process works best when the actions of everyone in the organisation are aligned with the strategy. Because of this, if you are not a strategic leader and still want to make a significant contribution to your organisation's strategy, you have to be careful in your approach. The starting point will usually be understanding what your organisation's strategy is (as well as what it ought to be). It is difficult to not engage in counterproductive actions, let alone make an above average contribution to realising the organisation's strategy, if you do not know what it is. The second step would be to understand how you can best contribute to this strategy within your current role as well as beyond your current role. To understand the strategy and how you can best contribute to it, you can review the available information on what the organisation's strategy is and how you can best contribute to it. You can also ask managers and strategic leaders to help you better understand the strategy and how you can best contribute to it. True leaders are likely to be more than happy to support you to fully understand it, as this is an important part of their job. Armed with this knowledge, you can then pursue the actions that best maximise your contribution to the organisation's strategy. If you believe the organisation's strategy isn't right or it is missing something, you can propose this to your line managers or to strategic leaders. They may help reinforce the core strategy messaging or incorporate your ideas to help refine the existing strategy.

Notes

1 Okumus, F. (2003). A framework to implement strategies in organizations. *Management Decision, 41*(9), 871–882.
2 Burgelman, R. A., & Grove, A. S. (2007). Let chaos reign, then reign in chaos – repeatedly: Managing strategic dynamics for corporate longevity. *Strategic Management Journal, 28*(10), 964–979.
3 Martin, R. (2014, June). Strategy is iterative prototyping. *Harvard Business Review.* Retrieved from https://hbr.org/2014/06/strategy-is-iterative-prototyping

4 Davis, J., Eisenhardt, K. M., & Bingham, C. B. (2009). Optimal structure, market dynamism, and the strategy of simple rules. *Administrative Science Quarterly, 54*, 413–452.
5 Wills, D. (2012). Probe into Flinders Medical Centre delays after paramedics protest over latest ramping, The Advertiser, May 8, Retrieved from https://www.adelaidenow.com.au/news/south-australia/paramedics-refusing-patient-billing-information-in-ramping-protest-to-cost-sa-government-200000-a-day-protest/story-e6frea83-1226349594673.
6 Busulwa, R. (2016). Strategy execution and complexity. University of South Australia. Retrieved from http://search.ror.unisa.edu.au/record/UNISA_ALMA11149688600001831/media/digital/open/9916160109801831/12149688590001831/13149688580001831/pdf

4 The Execution Premium Process

Origin and design principles

Origin

The Execution Premium Process was developed by Dr Robert Kaplan and Dr David Norton. Kaplan, a professor emeritus of leadership development at Harvard Business School, and Norton, a former KPMG partner and co-founder of the Palladium Group, are best known for their work advancing the Balanced Scorecard – a tool for linking a company's actions with its long-term goals.[1] They drew on their work on the Balanced Scorecard to develop the six-step closed loop Execution Premium Process, which outlines the key steps, activities and tools organisations can use to create competitive advantage and a better link between their strategy and operations.

The problem

Prior to Kaplan and Norton's work on the Balanced Scorecard, there had been a growing unease regarding the growing disconnect between financial measures and contemporary measures of business performance.[2] A key debate at the time was whether traditional financial measures were still relevant or whether operational performance measures were more important.[3] It was in this context that Kaplan and Norton introduced the Balanced Scorecard as a tool to integrate financial and operational measures so as to provide a comprehensive view of the business and a more forward-looking "leading view" of performance. The Balanced Scorecard evolved to provide guidance on the cause and effect linkages between different operational and financial measures and their relationship to the organisation's strategy. In their research and consulting work on applications of the Balanced Scorecard, Kaplan and Norton then observed a disconnect between strategy processes and operational processes – where an emphasis on one at the expense of the other often hampered organisation performance. For example, where development of strategic plans and operational plans occurred in silos, this often resulted in either strategic initiatives disrupting operations or the pursuit of operational targets sidelining strategic initiatives. They introduced the Execution Premium Process to align strategy and operational processes as a way to resolve this disconnect.

The idea in brief

The key steps in the Execution Premium Process are as follows[4]: (1) developing the strategy, (2) translating the strategy, (3) aligning organisation units and employees with the strategy, (4) planning operations by setting priorities for process management and allocating resources to deliver the strategy, (5) monitoring and learning from operations and strategy, and finally (6) testing and adapting the strategy. Kaplan and Norton unpack each step in the process and outline the objectives, key activities and tools to use to carry out each step. In unpacking each step, their process is one of the most comprehensive and prescriptive strategy execution processes (see Figure 4.1).

Step 1: Develop the strategy – This step seeks to have a clear mission, vision and values for the organisation and clear strategic objectives for the organisation to pursue. To achieve this, Kaplan and Norton propose that strategic leaders first undertake a review or reaffirmation of their organisation's mission, vision and values. Proceeding from this, they should then undertake strategic analysis (internal and external analysis) to identify their organisation's strengths, weakness, opportunities and threats (SWOT). Armed with this information, they can then formulate the strategy, that is, devise clear strategic objectives for the organisation to pursue that leverage strengths to seize opportunities, guard against threats and mitigate the effects of weaknesses.

Step 2: Plan the strategy – In this step, strategic leaders first clarify≈the cause and effect logic behind the strategic objectives and operations. One way to do this is by using the Balanced Scorecard to create Strategy Maps that visually represent the strategy and outline the causal linkages between strategy elements.[5] These linkages are typically organised using the four perspectives of the Balanced Scorecard (i.e. financial, customer, internal process and learning and growth). Then, measures of success for each strategic objective are determined and used to set the targets to be achieved in order to realise strategic

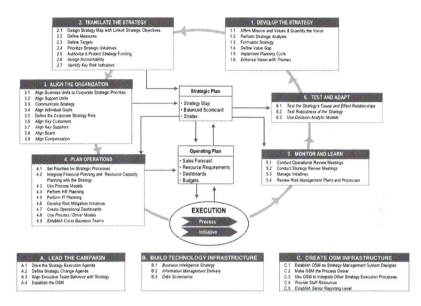

Figure 4.1 The Execution Premium Process.

objectives. Strategic initiatives or projects for the achievement of particular targets can then be devised and prioritised for achievement (e.g. which initiative is pursued first, which is dependent on other initiatives first being realised, when is it most effective to pursue each initiative etc.). Because strategic initiatives usually consume current resources that deliver future benefits and are therefore often eliminated when short-term pressures arise, Kaplan and Norton propose the allocation of separate funding outside of the operational budget and protection of this budget (i.e. Strategic Expense, or STRATEX budget). This is essential to ensure that strategic initiatives don't unintentionally draw resources away from operations, thus disrupting operations, and vice versa. Finally, they propose assignment of accountability for the achievement of strategic objectives and initiatives. Where strategic initiatives or targets are closely related, Kaplan and Norton propose bringing these under one umbrella or "theme" and assembling "theme teams" to lead execution of these groups of initiatives. For example, an organisation may have an innovation theme team to lead the pursuit of innovation-focused targets and strategic initiatives.

Step 3: Align the organisation – In Step 3, the organisation's business units, support units, employees and key stakeholders are aligned to strategic objectives. Key stakeholders can include key governance/advisory/oversight committees, key suppliers, key customers or key regulatory bodies. One way business units, support units, employees and other stakeholders can be aligned is through the creation scorecards aligned with the strategy. For example, business unit, support unit, employee and key stakeholder Balanced Scorecards can be created, outlining how each of these groups' activities contribute to the strategy and the targets they should achieve to realise this contribution to the strategy. At the most granular level, individual employee scorecards outline the targets each employee must achieve for the strategy to be realised. In this step, Kaplan and Norton also propose that the organisation's compensation systems be aligned with strategic objectives so that compensation systems incentivise the achievement of strategic objectives' targets and create disincentives to derailing attitudes, behaviours and actions.

Step 4: Plan operations – This step aims to have a clear operating plan for the organisation. Realising this begins with identifying and planning for the improvement of key processes critical to executing the strategy. Then, operational planning processes and outputs are configured for optimum support of the strategy. That is, capital and operating budgets, sales forecasts, resource capacity plans, HR plans, IT plans and other operational plans are all configured for the most efficient and effective realisation of the strategy.[6] For example, the IT plan may be configured for IT to play a greater role in the enablement of strategy communication and strategy monitoring through provision of efficient and effective platforms for carrying out these activities. Usually, the operating plan's scorecards or dashboards will show the cause and effect linkages between particular operational measures and targets and the strategy.

Step 5: Monitor and learn – In this step, operational review meetings are held to review and respond to operational data as well as to emerging operational issues. Strategy review meetings are also held to review the progress to the strategy and to respond to emerging strategic issues (e.g. due to changes in the internal and external environment).

Step 6: Test and adapt – In the final step, strategy testing and adapting meetings are held to assess performance of the strategy and the consequences of changes in the environment.

As with the 7 Factor Process, the Execution Premium Process also requires significant strategic leadership involvement to be effective. Kaplan and Norton propose that strategic leaders should define and drive the strategic change agenda and the strategy execution agenda. Further, they should ensure alignment of executive team behaviour with the strategy and establish an Office of Strategy Management (OSM)[7] to oversee and facilitate the Execution Premium Process activities. As part of establishing the OSM, strategic leaders should ensure this office has adequate authority, resources and accountability to be the process designer, facilitator and owner. Finally, Kaplan and Norton propose that the Execution Premium Process ought to be supported by appropriate technology infrastructure to enable adequate business intelligence, information management and data governance.

Caveats

Despite first appearances, the originators of the Execution Premium Process do not propose that strategy execution is neat, linear and sequential or that strategy formation and implementation are different and separate phases of strategy realisation. Rather, the key activities identified should be taken as iterative processes that happen in organisations every day. For example, Steps 5 and 6, "Monitor and Learn" and "Test and Adapt", are the continuous tasks of leaders who wish to ensure that operational issues don't disrupt the strategy, that obstacles to the strategy are identified and resolved in a timely manner and that the strategy is adapted to real-time changes in the internal and external environment.

What you might know it as

If you have gone through contemporary business schools or absorbed much of the traditional business literature, most elements of the Execution Premium Process are likely to seem familiar. This is because each step essentially synthesised and integrated the existing strategy formation, strategic planning and strategy implementation body of knowledge in existence at that time. The unpacking of each step also synthesised and integrated established activities and tools. For example, Step 1, "Develop the Strategy", unpacks into traditional strategy formulation activities such as undertaking internal and external analysis, and these activities are, in turn, carried out using established tools such as Porter's 5 Forces Analysis, Value Chain Analysis and the SWOT matrix. If you are familiar with the 7 Factor Process, you may also see significant similarities between these two processes, albeit much less prescription in the 7 Factor Process as far as the specific activities to achieve each step and the specific tools to use to carry out activities. Users of the Balanced Scorecard will also be familiar with many elements of the Execution Premium Process such as "translating the strategy into objectives and measures" and "aligning the organisation through cascading of the corporate or organisation Balanced Scorecard".

Prevalence

Across all sectors, we found 18 per cent of organisations, or almost one in every five organisations, using the Execution Premium Process to execute strategy. While this process was used across all sectors, it was most commonly cited by large corporate, government and NGO/NFP organisations. Within the private sector, we found that the bigger the organisation the more often the Execution Premium Process was used. Organisations with more than 500 employees cited the greatest use of the process, closely followed by organisations with 51–499 employees. The Execution Premium Process was strongly associated with high execution effectiveness in obvious, complicated and complex but low volatility environments. But across all environments, more than half of organisations making extensive use of this process cited high execution effectiveness relative to peers. Across all sectors and organisation sizes, the Execution Premium Process was one of the most commonly known and cited processes (see Figure 4.2).

The process in action

To demonstrate the Execution Premium Process in action, what follows is the case study of large multinational organisation' adoption, implementation and use of the Execution Premium Process to execute strategy. As you read the case, pay attention to how the organisation approaches each step of the Execution Premium Process as well as

	Sector				Employees (Org Size)				
Process	Public Sector / Government	Private Sector	NGO/NFP	All Sectors	>500	51-499	2 - 50	<2	All Sizes
7 Factor Process	10%	13%	25%	13%	19%	10%	10%	0%	12%
Execution Premium Process	24%	16%	25%	18%	25%	21%	13%	11%	18%
Simple Rules	14%	20%	17%	18%	13%	21%	23%	44%	21%
Lean Strategy Deployment Process	14%	19%	25%	18%	22%	21%	15%	11%	18%
Change Acceleration Process	14%	11%	17%	12%	9%	21%	10%	11%	12%
Project Management Process	53%	80%	66%	70%	88%	84%	63%	33%	72%
Talent Placement Process	14%	27%	25%	23%	22%	26%	23%	11%	22%
Outcomes and Incentives / Disincentives Communication Process	24%	28%	25%	26%	31%	26%	25%	11%	26%
Learning on the Run Process	39%	38%	50%	38%	31%	42%	43%	22%	37%
Resource Allocation / Portfolio Management Process	19%	17%	25%	18%	22%	21%	18%	66%	24%
Performance Monitoring and Feedback Process	39%	38%	50%	38%	44%	37%	43%	0%	38%

Figure 4.2 Proportion of study participants citing use of the Execution Premium Process by sector and organisation size.

Note: *For example, of the 241 study participants, 50 participants were from the public sector/government. Of these 50 public sector/government participants, 5 participants (10%) used the 7 Factor Process. This table differs from Tables 6.23 and 6.24 shown in Busulwa (2016), where process users in each sector are shown as a proportion of all study participants.

how it carries out the activities within that step and the tools it uses to carry out the different steps and activities. Also consider the organisation's unique context, the challenges of this context for the Execution Premium Process and how the organisation overcomes these challenges to realise the benefits of using the Execution Premium Process. As you review the case, if you believe the Execution Premium Process suits your organisation's unique context, you may be able to adapt some of the approaches in the case study to your organisation's approach to the process. Alternatively, you may decide that the process is not suited to your particular organisation; in which case, one or more of the other processes in this book may be more suitable. Still, there may be particular strategy execution insights and practices that you can pick up and adapt to whatever process you choose to use.

Case study: Merck & Co's "Plan to Win": strategy execution at a global pharmaceutical giant[8]

Merck & Co is the second largest pharmaceutical firm in the world. It operates in more than 140 countries with products and service lines that range from vaccines and prescription drugs to over-the-counter allergy medications. Merck & Co employs more than 90,000 people and has a turnover of more than $50 billion.

Merck & Co has clear and longstanding mission, vision and values. In 2005, it undertook external and internal strategic analysis to develop its strategy. This analysis revealed that a number of events had recently converged to create a daunting business environment. These included governments making drug reimbursements more difficult, a large number of the company's patents becoming due to expire, innovation becoming riskier and more costly and increasing regulatory scrutiny. Looking ahead 5 years to 2010, the company was anticipating losing up to $10 billion in revenue, and industry analysts had ranked it near the bottom of leading healthcare companies. But the company had strengths it could build on, including a talented global workforce, a range of innovative product offerings worldwide and a strong commitment to R&D investment.

Drawing on its clear mission, vision and values and findings from its strategic analysis, Merck & Co developed its strategy and dubbed it "Plan to Win". The strategy fit into six key focus areas: improving customer value, innovation, differentiated prescriptions, effective and efficient commercialisation, a lean and flexible business model and a high-performance culture. Once it had developed the strategy, Merck & Co heeded the findings of its internal strategic analysis, which suggested that successfully executing the strategy would require major changes across the company. For instance, previously independent support functions and business services would need to be centralised to improve service, create new efficiencies, promote timelier decision-making and produce clearer lines of accountability. The company determined it would need to rebuild its strategy execution infrastructure to support the execution of the strategy.

In 2005, the company moved to implement the Balanced Scorecard as a platform for improving how the following Execution Premium Process steps were carried out: planning the strategy, linking strategy to operations, aligning organisational units and employees and monitoring and learning from progress of strategy execution. The company followed this by establishing a Strategy Realisation Office (SRO) in 2006 (Merck's version of the OSM). The SRO was charged with the mandate of translating Merck & Co's strategy into a corporate strategy map and scorecard with clear measures and targets. The SRO ensured that Merck & Co's corporate strategy map and scorecard identified a clear initiatives portfolio with clear objectives, measures, targets and accountability for delivering on each initiative and target. The SRO eventually came to report to the CEO, and had leadership of these key Execution Premium Process activities: developing, testing and adapting the strategy; allocating resources for initiatives; and managing scorecard reporting and strategy reviews. Later, Merck & Co augmented its SRO with the Project Realisation Office (PRO) and charged the PRO with fostering alignment across strategic initiative teams, sharing best practices and addressing strategic risk at the local level.

With leadership from the SRO and PRO, Merck & Co aligned organisation units and employees through division, support function and individual scorecards all aligned with the strategy. After implementing individual scorecards, Merck was able to align employee incentives for the delivery of "threshold" and "stretch" targets. These efforts resolved issues of too many measures and unaligned measures and incentives.

To undertake step 4 of the Execution Premium Process, Merck created divisional and functional PROs and charged them with managing and analysing their operational information and reviewing it each month with their leadership team and executive committee member. The SRO was then charged with analysing the information with the executive committee before each quarterly strategy review. This structure cascaded to divisions and support functions who used scorecards to conduct their own operational reviews.

Merck & Co's efforts to put in place the strategy execution infrastructure to carry out all the steps and activities in the Execution Premium Process paid dividends. Between 2005 and 2010, worldwide sales grew from $22 billion to $46 billion, its share price rose from $28.05 to $36.04 and its earnings per share rose from $2.53 to $3.42. Further, its Harris Interactive Reputation Quotient rose by 5.2 points, its clinical cycle times improved 7 per cent and its retention of high performing and high potential employees improved 3.6 per cent.

Are you in the right environment for this process?

We found the Execution Premium Process to be most effective in obvious, complicated and complex but low volatility environments. Therefore, if you are in a high velocity or high volatility environment or in an organisation undergoing rapid transformation, then you are not in the right environment for this process. The Execution Premium Process was also found to be most commonly used in large corporate, government and NGO/NFP organisations. If these organisation types and environments are similar to your organisation, then the Execution Premium will likely work well at your organisation. But there are other issues to consider. Your organisation must be in a position to commit the significant resources required to carry out the different steps and activities of the Execution Premium Process. For instance, we noted earlier that the OSM alone may require six or more full-time staff. Further, significant resources are required to develop the strategy, translate it, cascade it, align the whole organisation and carry out regular strategy and operational reviews. Usually, use of the Execution Premium Process also requires significant reconfigurations of the organisation's systems and process infrastructure. Finally, as Kaplan and Norton point out, strategic leaders must have the motivation, time and bandwidth to define and drive the strategic change agenda and the strategy execution agenda as well as to ensure ongoing alignment of executive team behaviour with the strategy.

Knowing when you are using it

You are likely to be using the Execution Premium Process if the six steps described earlier resemble the steps taken by your organisation to execute strategy. Other telltale indicators include the structure and formality of your strategy process, use of the Balanced Scorecard and related tools such as Strategy Maps and corporate scorecards cascaded to business and functional units. You might also observe routine operations review and strategy review meetings occurring. If your organisation has a strategy management office, this is also an indication you may be using this process. Usually, you will hear the use of terminology such as "strategic initiatives", "Strategy Maps", "alignment", "scorecards", "Strategic Expenditure" and other terms described earlier.

Process strengths and shortcomings

We observed three key strengths of the Execution Premium Process. The first is its prescriptiveness. As we noted earlier, it is one of the first processes to fully unpack the strategic management process into clear activities, roles and tools for the realisation of strategy. In doing so, it provides very clear guidance on how to execute strategy. While it can be argued there are some downsides to being overly prescriptive, overall we believe this is a strength in certain circumstances. A second strength of this process is its incorporation of the traditional strategic management body of knowledge and tools. This is a strength because it builds on the concepts, processes, tools and language that most stakeholders within an organisation are likely to be familiar with. As such, it would likely be consistent with existing logics within most organisations regarding how strategy is realised and result in less resistance to the use of the Execution Premium Process. Third, there are numerous case studies, established practice groups and thought leadership groups as well as established consulting services that can be drawn on in the use of the Execution Premium Process. For example, leaders can issue the Execution Premium books, case studies or white papers as resources for people on their teams to get up to speed on particular roles, activities and tools of the process.

For organisations using this process, the most cited frustration areas or perceived barriers to better strategy execution included lack of strategy consultation or bottom up input into the strategy, inadequate engagement building, insufficient purpose building and insufficient strategy justification or rationale building. Employees, particularly from middle management to the front line, wanted to have some input into the strategy rather than just having senior managers formulate the strategy top down. Moving beyond formation of the strategy, they wanted to be clear on their roles in strategy execution and to remain better apprised of the progress of strategy execution efforts. They also wanted a clear rationale for pursuing a particular strategy. Finally, they wanted to be clear on the overarching purpose for doing what they did every day: in other words, to have a clear and compelling purpose. These are areas that strategic leaders using this particular process can dedicate more personal attention to in order to better catalyse strategy execution.

Other challenges of this process include its resource intensity. To carry out all the steps and activities may require more resources than most organisations are able to procure. For instance, we noted earlier that the OSM alone may require six or more full-time staff. That's before considering resources that may be required to develop, cascade, align and review progress towards the different objectives and targets. It is perhaps for this reason that we found the process to be most in use in large organisations capable of expending such resources. The fact that the processes essentially reach every part of the organisation to ensure alignment with and contribution to the strategy also means that a significant amount of effort may have to be expended on communicating the strategy and building organisation-wide buy-in into the strategy and the execution process. A final challenge of this process is that a reasonable level of internal and external stability and reasonably long strategy refresh windows may be required. That is, it may prove very difficult to use in environments under constant change and disruption.

Common tips and traps

As previously discussed, a common trap with any process is to see it and attempt to use it as a sequential process with each step awaiting the full completion of the prior step before beginning. Instead, the Execution Premium Process should be seen and used as an iterative process, with each step and all steps collectively operating as ongoing iterative processes of prototyping, testing, modification and retesting until strategy is realised.[9] This enables faster strategy refresh, timely issue identification and course correction and thus better adaptation to internal and external environment changes. Another trap common to many processes is to attempt to use this process without adequate buy-in and leadership from the CEO and the top management team or dominant coalitions. Adequate buy-in and leadership from these groups are fundamental to the process' initiation, implementation and functioning.

While these traps are generic, there are also some common traps unique to the Execution Premium Process. The first of these is attempting to use this process in environments not suited to it without adapting its use to the unique challenges of those environments. Such environments include high velocity or high volatility environments, those undergoing significant disruption, environments with unstable leadership and environments with unstable organisation structures. In such environments, it is likely that critical steps or activities in the Execution Premium Process will experience bottlenecks, get derailed and in turn derail the whole process. For example, an unstable top management team is likely to result in weak strategic leadership, whereas strong strategic leadership from the CEO and the top management team or dominant coalition is necessary to effectively lead the strategy execution agenda and process.

Another common trap unique to the Execution Premium Process is having insufficient resources to use this process. We noted earlier that some organisations may not be able to commit the necessary financial, people, time and technology resources required to fully utilise this process and realise its benefits. When this is the case, failed implementation of the process or unrealised strategic initiatives are the likely results of efforts to use the process. Also, because significant resources are required to use the process and it is not an overnight implementation, prospective users ought to have long-term intentions for use of this process. Using it briefly and then abandoning it is likely to result in significant waste (usually from the upfront finance, people, time and technology infrastructure required to implement it prior to using it to realise strategy). In highlighting the common traps, our intention is not to discourage use of any process but rather to point to the areas prospective or current process users need to pay attention to and what they can do more effectively to use the particular process.

Spotlight on the role of strategic leaders

While strong strategic leadership maximises the efficiency and effectiveness of all processes, it is fundamental to the functioning of the Execution Premium Process. First, it is essential to getting adequate resources to implement this process. Strategic leaders wanting to realise the full benefits of this process ought to get involved early in making the case for use of this process, fighting for adequate resources to implement the process so the implementation is not set up for failure and engaging the whole organisation on the business value of the processes. Then, it is essential for them to define the strategic change agenda, to drive the strategy execution agenda, to align the top management team or dominant coalitions' behaviours to the strategy, to invest in the necessary technology and process infrastructure and to establish, empower and institutionalise the OSM infrastructure. Without these essential strategic leadership roles, this process is likely to result in failed initiatives, if its implementation gets off the ground to begin with.

We asked executive, middle management and front-line employees at organisations using this process about their frustrations with strategy execution. The most common frustrations included power brokers not supporting the strategy, the strategy not being clearly explained and justified, lack of a clear and compelling purpose for the organisation, insufficient communication of the strategy, insufficient consultation/ bottom up input into the strategy and having inadequate IT infrastructure to support the strategy. When not sufficiently and effectively addressed, these issues can sap morale and undermine strategy execution efforts. As such, another essential role of strategic leaders is to be vigilant to these issues and ensure strategy execution is led in such a way as to resolve these issues and optimise execution effectiveness.

What if you are not a strategic leader?

If you are not a strategic leader but want to maximise your contribution to the organisation's strategy, there are three important steps you can take. The first step is to make sure you understand the strategy, that is, understand what the strategy is, the rationale for that strategy and why it is better than alternate strategies that could have been used. Once you have understood your organisation's strategy, then it would be best to understand how you can best contribute to the strategy both in your current role and beyond your current role, that is, understand how your job contributes to the strategy, what actions you can take to make a stronger contribution to the strategy and what behaviours and values you can model to best contribute to the strategy. To understand the strategy and how you can best contribute to it, you can review the available information on what the organisation's strategy is and how you can best contribute to it. Such information may be available on the organisation's website, in documents on the organisation's website, on other online sites and in strategy communications from the top management team. You can also ask managers and strategic leaders to help you better understand the strategy and how you can best contribute to it. They are likely to be more than happy to support you to fully understand it, as this is one of the more important parts of their job. Having taken these first two steps, you will be in a position to ensure that any actions and behaviours you engage in actually support the strategy rather than derail it. This may seem obvious, but without an understanding of the strategy and how to best contribute to it, you are more likely to just maintain the status quo at best and to engage in counterproductive actions and behaviours at worst. But equipped with knowledge of the strategy and how you can best contribute to it, you are equipped for the third step. The third step is to ensure you engage in all the attitudes and behaviours that best support the strategy, and then take all the actions within your power that you have confirmed maximise your contribution to the strategy.

Notes

1 Kaplan, R. S., & Norton, D. P. (1996). Using the balanced scorecard as a strategic management system. *Harvard Business Review, 74*(1), 75–85.
2 Kaplan, R. S., & Johnson, H. T. (1987). *Relevance lost: The rise and fall of management accounting.* Boston, MA: Harvard Business School Press.
3 Johnson, H. T. (2002). *Relevance regained.* New York, NY: Simon and Schuster.
4 Kaplan, R. S., & Norton, D. P. (2008). *The execution premium: Linking strategy to operations for competitive advantage.* Boston, MA: Harvard Business School Publishing.
5 Kaplan, R. S., Kaplan, R. E., Norton, D. P., Norton, D. P., & Davenport, T. H. (2004). *Strategy maps: Converting intangible assets into tangible outcomes.* Chicago, IL: Harvard Business Press.
6 Kaplan, R. S., & Norton, D. P. (2008). *The execution premium: Linking strategy to operations for competitive advantage.* Boston, MA: Harvard Business School Publishing.
7 Kaplan, R., & Norton, D. (2005). *The office of strategy management. Harvard Business Review, 87*(4), 8.
8 Palladium Group (2011). *Strategy execution champions: The palladium balanced scorecard hall of fame report 2011.* Boston, MA: Harvard Business School Press.
9 Martin, R. (2014, June). Strategy is iterative prototyping. *Harvard Business Review.* Retrieved from https://hbr.org/2014/06/strategy-is-iterative-prototyping

5 The Hoshin Planning or Lean Strategy Deployment Process

Origin and design principles

Origin

Lean Strategy Deployment (also referred to as Hoshin Planning, Hoshin Kanri, Direction Management or Policy Deployment) is a process for forming and actioning "breakthroughs" that significantly change the position of an organisation in its external environment through strategically aligned business objectives and metrics that are driven from both top-down and bottom-up activity. Originating as Hoshin Planning, this process emerged out of efforts that drove Japan's dramatic transformation and rebuild following the Second World War. Hoshin Planning was brought together and developed from a combination of Miyamoto Musashi's teachings used to guide samurai warriors, Joseph M. Juran's teachings about management's role in leading quality improvement efforts, W. Edwards Deming's teachings about quality management and the Plan–Do–Check–Act (PDCA) cycle and lessons learned from companies participating in the Deming Prize in Japan. It also incorporated some of Peter Drucker's work on management by objectives. In 1965, Bridgestone Tire analysed and published a report on the planning techniques of companies winning the Deming Prize. These techniques were given the name Hoshin Kanri (or Hoshin Planning, in English). They became widely accepted and used in Japan by 1975. By the early 1980s, Hoshin Planning had spread into some pockets of the United States, mainly introduced from Japanese-based subsidiaries of US companies that were winners of the Deming Prize. This included, for example, Japanese subsidiaries of Fuji Xerox and Hewlett-Packard. But Hoshin Planning was not greatly shared amongst US organisations, as companies considered it a secret source of competitive advantage and did not want to share it. Its spread was partially catalysed by the success of Lean Manufacturing and the growing interest in and adoption of Lean principles and concepts outside of manufacturing. It is largely through adoption of Lean principles and concepts that Hoshin Planning has reached mainstream adoption.

The problem

Japan undertook a dramatic transformation and rebuild agenda following the Second World War. During this period, Japanese firms looked far and wide for ideas on how to deliver significant performance breakthroughs. This included ideas on how to solve the emerging and critical management challenges of the time such as improving quality, minimising waste, aligning different levels of the organisation and ensuring the flow of ideas, both top-down and bottom-up. Hoshin Planning evolved as a response to these issues and offered organisations a vehicle for making and sustaining dramatic performance breakthroughs. It has further evolved with the evolution in Lean principles and concepts to be referred to as Lean Strategy Deployment.

The idea in brief

The key steps in the Lean Strategy Deployment or Hoshin Planning Process are[1] the following: (1) establish a clear organisation vision, (2) develop 3–5-year breakthrough objectives, (3) develop annual objectives, (4) deploy annual objectives, (5) implement annual objectives, (6) undertake regular progress review and (7) undertake annual review. Hoshin Planning practitioners and researchers unpack each step in the process and outline the objectives of each step as well as the different ways those objectives can be achieved (see Figure 5.1).

Step 1: Establish a clear organisation vision – This step seeks to specify the future aspirations of the firm to its stakeholders and to set out a compelling rationale for this direction. To achieve this, Hoshin Planning researchers and practitioners propose starting with strategic analysis of the organisation's internal and external environment. In doing so, strategic leaders will be in a better position to determine the organisation's current situation (or "current state") and its resultant opportunities and threats. Having determined the organisation's opportunities and threats, strategic leaders will then have a stronger basis for providing a compelling rationale for change, to outline the desired vision (or "future state") and explain the rationale for it.

Step 2: Develop 3–5-year breakthrough objectives – Breakthrough objectives are statements that succinctly crystalise the critical 3–5-year

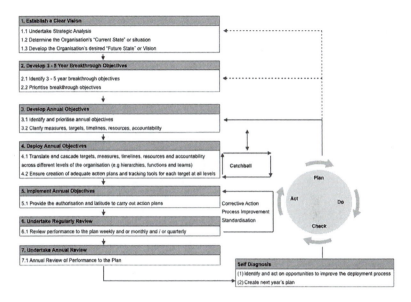

Figure 5.1 The Hoshin Planning or Lean Strategy Deployment Process.

achievements necessary to realise the organisation's vision.[2] While a range of such objectives can initially be identified, Lean Strategy Deployment researchers propose prioritising three to five breakthrough objectives to sharpen the organisation's focus.[3] Breakthrough objectives are typically developed in sessions attended by the organisation's leader, her direct reports and critical support team members (e.g. finance, HR, IT). In these sessions, ideas for breakthrough objectives are brainstormed, debated, refined, prioritised and reprioritized until a final list of four to five breakthrough objectives are decided on. Open and honest debate as well as leadership team maturity is usually essential to arrive at objectives with strong buy-in and commitment. An example of a breakthrough objective at one point for GE Healthcare was "Create an inspirational culture, drawing the best from our legacy businesses and melding it into the highest performing team in America's service: Sharing Passion for Success".[4]

Step 3: Develop annual objectives – In this step, similar sessions to Step 2 are held to answer the question: What do we need to achieve this year in order to achieve our breakthrough objectives in the next 3–5 years? Through engaged brainstorming, constructive debate, refinement and prioritisation, each of the breakthrough objectives is broken down into the vital few annual objectives essential to its achievement over the next 3–5 years. For example, one of GE Healthcare's annual objectives at the time was "Implement new processes to identify and forever resolve employee dissatisfiers". Measures, targets, delivery timeframes, resources and accountability for delivery of each annual objective are also typically debated and clarified in these sessions to develop and prioritise the annual objectives.

Step 4: Deploy annual objectives – This step is concerned with how to translate and cascade annual objectives to all parts of the organisation, for example, across all parts of the hierarchy, across all functions and across all parts of the value chain. There are a range of approaches and tools that can be used to achieve this. Typically, each manager conducts continuous "catchball" dialogue with their direct reports about the targets being allocated to them, what resources are required to achieve those targets and the opportunities or barriers to achieving those targets. For example, if the organisation's head of customer experience was allocated the annual objective of "Achieving a 10 per cent improvement in the organisation's Net Promoter score", she may deploy this objective through "catchball" dialogues or debates with her team members about what they each need to achieve for her to achieve her annual objective, what obstacles they face and what financial or non-financial resources they each need in order to achieve their targets. Her team members can in turn undertake the same process with their teams, thus deploying (i.e. translating and cascading) the objective.

Step 5: Implement annual objectives – In this step, action is taken to realise the annual objectives. This usually involves assigned leaders of each target meeting with their teams on a regular basis to create the detailed who/what/when action plans for achieving the target, authorising and providing their teams with the latitude and resources to act on those action plans, tracking progress and course correcting as necessary until the target is achieved. Lean and Hoshin Planning researchers and practitioners prescribe a range of tools and techniques that can be used in this step. For example, bowling charts can be used to visually track implementation progress. And Deming's PDCA[5] system can be used to diagnose and resolve implementation issues, as well as to incorporate them into modification of current or future objectives or how these are deployed. Other tools and techniques such as Kaizen events,[6] DMAIC,[7] A3[8] forms and bowling charts can be used for implementation (e.g. see Figure 5.2).

Step 6: Undertake regular progress reviews – An all too common occurrence in many organisations is that they invest a whole lot

Figure 5.2 Bowling chart tracking planned versus actual progress of an annual objective action plan at GE Healthcare.[9]

of time in forming strategy, only to find at year's end that it has been sidelined by unexpected or emergent crises and the ongoing pressures of day-to-day operations. Thus, Step 6 of the Hoshin Planning Process helps to avoid this trap through regular review of each person's progress towards targets and action plans, and identification and resolution of execution barriers, to ensure that forward progress is maintained. Regular reviews can occur daily, weekly, monthly, quarterly or as often as is needed for timely corrective actions to be taken.

Step 7: Undertake annual progress review – At the end of the year, a thorough review is undertaken to determine how far ahead or behind the organisation is against its objectives and what adjustments need to be made in the coming year. For example, it may be necessary to adjust 3–5-year objectives or the next year's annual objectives. During this process, resource allocation issues from the completed year are also considered for any lessons to ensure resources are properly allocated for what needs to be accomplished in the coming year.

Caveats

Similar to other processes, the literature does not propose that this process is neat, linear and sequential or that strategy formation is a different and separate phase to strategy realisation. Thus, we propose taking it as an iterative process with each step able to occur or be revised in real time as demanded by the organisation's environment. For instance, it may be that halfway through the year, some of the annual objectives are rendered irrelevant by surprising changes in the organisation's external or internal environment. Where this occurs, the leader of the organisation and their team should undertake the relevant steps in the Hoshin Planning Process to ensure relevant breakthrough objectives with corresponding targets, measures, resources and ownership replace those rendered obsolete. This better positions the organisation to adapt in a timely manner to its external environment as opposed to waiting until the upcoming annual objectives in order to adapt to the change.

What you might know it as

If you have been involved in quality improvement initiatives such as the introduction of Lean or Six Sigma within an organisation, you may have come across many of the steps within the Hoshin Planning Process. Depending on your location within the organisation hierarchy or the value chain, you may have had greater exposure to particular Hoshin Planning concepts and tools such as PDCA or A3. If you are a senior manager involved in Lean or Six Sigma activities, you are likely to have been involved in discussions about linking quality improvement efforts to strategy. Many organisations have established strategy execution processes which operate in parallel with quality and process improvement methods. Where this is the case, such processes may already stipulate annual objectives but may then apply process improvement methods for the achievement of process improvement targets.[10] In such cases, you may have only been exposed to Step 4 onwards. Alternatively, you may know many of the steps of the Hoshin Planning Process as prescribed success factors for using Lean or Six Sigma methodologies.[11] Finally, you may find that particular process improvement or quality improvement consulting groups have adapted the Hoshin Planning Process steps into their own proprietary versions of the process. In these situations, the language and terminology used may differ, but you should notice parallels between the activities and steps they describe and the steps and activities we described earlier.

Prevalence

Across all sectors, we found 18 per cent of organisations, or one in every five organisations, using the Lean Strategy Deployment or Hoshin Planning Process. While used across all sectors, the process was most commonly cited by the NGO/NFP sector (25%) and the private sector, although the public sector/government use was not far behind (14%). In general, we found that the bigger the organisation, the more likely it was that the Lean Strategy Deployment process was in use. Organisations with more than 500 employees cited the greatest use of the process, closely followed by organisations with 51–499 employees. The process was cited to be more effective at realising deliberate rather

	Sector				Employees (Org Size)			
Process	Public Sector / Government	Private Sector	NGO/NFP	All Sectors	>500	51-499	2 - 50	<2	All Sizes
7 Factor Process	10%	13%	25%	13%	19%	10%	10%	0%	12%
Execution Premium Process	24%	16%	25%	18%	25%	21%	13%	11%	18%
Simple Rules	14%	20%	17%	18%	13%	21%	23%	44%	21%
Lean Strategy Deployment Process	14%	19%	25%	18%	22%	21%	15%	11%	18%
Change Acceleration Process	14%	11%	17%	12%	9%	21%	10%	11%	12%
Project Management Process	53%	80%	66%	70%	86%	84%	63%	33%	72%
Talent Placement Process	14%	27%	25%	23%	22%	26%	23%	11%	22%
Outcomes and Incentives / Disincentives Communication Process	24%	28%	25%	26%	31%	26%	25%	11%	26%
Learning on the Run Process	39%	38%	50%	38%	31%	42%	43%	22%	37%
Resource Allocation / Portfolio Management Process	19%	17%	25%	18%	22%	21%	18%	66%	24%
Performance Monitoring and Feedback Process	39%	38%	50%	38%	44%	37%	43%	0%	38%

Figure 5.3 Proportion of study participants citing use of the Hoshin Planning Process by sector and organisation size.

Note: *For example, of the 241 study participants, 50 participants were from the public sector/government. Of these 50 public sector/government participants, 5 participants (10%) used the 7 Factor Process. This table differs from Tables 6.23 and 6.24 shown in Busulwa (2016), where process users in each sector are shown as a proportion of all study participants.

than emergent strategy and to have low execution effectiveness in high velocity, complex and chaotic environments (see Figure 5.3).

The process in action

To demonstrate the Hoshin Planning Process in action, we have used the case of a large healthcare system or network. Healthcare systems are well known for their structural complexity and competing professional and market logics. As you read the case, pay attention to how the organisation approaches each step of the process and the particular challenges it faces in doing so. Also consider the organisation's unique context, the challenges of this context for the Hoshin Planning Process and how the organisation overcomes these challenges. As you review the case, if you believe the process suits your organisation's unique context, you may be able to adapt some of the approaches in the case study to your organisation's unique approach to using the process. You may find that your organisation does not have the complexity of a large healthcare system, in which case each step is likely to be much simpler at your organisation. Alternatively, you may decide that the process is not well suited to your particular organisation, in which case one or more of the other processes in this book may be more suitable. However, there may be particular strategy execution insights and practices that you can pick up from the case study and adapt to whatever process your organisation uses.

Case study: Scott and White Healthcare: using Hoshin Planning to align 13,000 staff[12]

Scott and White Healthcare is a non-profit healthcare system that owns, partners or manages more than 11 acute care hospitals, more than 140 clinics and more than 70 primary care and speciality clinics. The organisation employs more than 14,000 employees with over 1,200 physicians. It is the largest multi-specialty practice in Texas and one of the largest multi-specialty practices in the United States. In 2008, Scott and White was going through significant growth, growing geographic dispersion of more than 29,000 square miles, facing significant healthcare reform, facing significant benefits/compensation changes and significant financial challenges. Senior leaders were clear on the organisation vision, goals and objectives but noticed a clear disconnect with front-line staff. They wanted to better align the different parts of the organisation and engage all staff around the vision and strategic objectives. They engaged Lean consultancy organisation Altarum Institute to support them in applying Lean to achieve this.

With Altarum's facilitation, senior leaders started their Lean Strategy Deployment journey by attending a lean certification program in May, offered by the University of Michigan. This provided sufficient knowledge of Lean thinking and Hoshin Planning principles, tools and practices, including 5S, A3 Problem Solving, Waste Walks and Strategy Deployment. Following this, senior leaders started by translating the vision and strategic objectives into the critical SMART (Specific, Measurable, Attainable, Realistic, and Time-bound) goals and went through "catchball" sessions with all executive team members to determine an accountable executive team member for each goal. Then, hospitals, clinics and support function areas were identified for piloting "catchball" dialogues with their area leaders about their cascaded targets and measures, the resources required to achieve those targets and barriers to achieving those targets. Learnings from the piloting phase were used to update the process and to update the tools used to carry out the "catchball" dialogues.

In June, senior management established a Council for Strategic Activation that included 450 physicians and business leaders. The objective of this group was to effectively communicate long-term and annual objectives and goals as well as the strategy deployment process, tools, training and timelines. All leaders were required to attend a 1-hour deployment process overview session which provided essential knowledge about cascading goals and targets and carrying out effective catchball sessions. These sessions were presented by four Altarum coaches and 12 previously trained internal coaches. A coach was assigned to every regional site to provide support, answer questions about the process, add tools and to help with resolving any issues.

In July, the catchball sessions began. Wave 1 comprised one-on-one sessions between senior leaders and the president/CEO to set and document their goals. A third-party "coach" facilitated each session. These sessions were then cascaded by having each senior leader going through the same process with their direct reports. The sessions were completed in August. In September, catchball cascade to all staff began with mass training sessions being delivered by ten master trainers and nine orientation trainers. Each staff member received an overview of the deployment process and received two assignments: to review their leader's goals within 7 days and to submit their own goals to contribute to the leader's goals within 30 days. A standardised form was issued for each staff member to use. By November, more than 90 per cent of all forms had been completed and submitted.

In December, the organisation began Steps 5 and 6 of the process. A goal alignment and target tracking excel template tool was established for use in monthly review conversations about progress to goals. These conversations were face-to-face between line managers and their staff. The conversations centred around four questions: What is your goal? How are you going with it? What's your plan? How can I help you? Annual review of the process effectiveness and lessons learned was also undertaken.

Scott and White Healthcare's results from using the Lean Strategy Deployment Process included, but weren't limited to, greater commitment from senior leaders and clinicians, greater engagement, revenue and productivity growth. Lessons learned from the experience of applying the Lean Strategy Deployment Process included the value to staff of taking unaligned tasks off their plate instead of just adding new ones, the benefits of joint CEO and Chief Medical Officer leadership to maintain clinician engagement, the benefits of having specialist Lean Strategy Deployment practitioners to support implementation of the process, the importance of allowing up to 1 hour per catchball session and up to three catchball sessions to finalise goals, not underestimating resistance and the importance of ensuring senior leadership support.

Are you in the right environment for this process?

In our data, there wasn't a standout environment for the Hoshin Planning Process. But in seeking to constrain actions not aligned to breakthrough objectives, the process does tend to favour the realisation of deliberate strategies. As such, it may be more effective in complicated but low volatility and complex but low velocity environments, though the data did not conclusively suggest this. In complicated environments, cause and effect is discoverable and thus accurate predictions about the future can be made. When this is the case, breakthrough objectives and corresponding annual objectives and action plans can be formed on the basis of the accurate predictions. For example, through sophisticated analysis, strategic leaders can anticipate externalities leading to crisis and form breakthrough objectives to best position the firm to weather the crisis or capitalise on it. Or alternatively, the crisis may not be predictable, but after the occurrence of certain events, strategic leaders may be able to determine the cause of these events and reconfigure the organisation's financial and operating model to be better equipped should those events (or worse) happen in future. You can check if you are in these types of environments by asking yourself how easy or difficult it is to determine cause and effect and to make accurate predictions in your organisation's environment. If it isn't very difficult to accurately determine the causes of events or to making accurate predictions, then your organisation is in a complicated or complex environment. If the rate of change is low to moderate, then you are likely in a complicated but low volatility or a complex but low velocity environment. In such a case, you may be in the right environment for the Hoshin Planning Process.

If you are in environments characterised by prediction difficulty and surprising events, a strategy process biased towards the realisation of emergent strategy may be more ideal. Such processes constrain the actions of employees less and thus encourage improvisation and the formation of autonomous strategies. One or more of these strategies is likely to be the vehicle for the organisation to adapt to unexpected changes in its environment. That being said, the Hoshin Planning Process can be adapted to loosen constraint on action. This can occur in how tightly breakthrough objectives are defined and in how objectives are deployed across different levels of the organisation. Action is most constrained when breakthrough objectives and their corresponding targets and action plans are tightly defined (e.g. the breakthrough objective "98 per cent of loans closed in 30 days"); and when the nature of catchball conversations is more along the lines of "here is your target/how do you plan to achieve it?". Constraint on action is loosened when objectives are broadly defined (e.g. "become a podium brand") and when the nature of catchball conversations is more along the lines of "what should our vision and breakthrough objectives be/how can you contribute to their achievement/what support do you need in order to make the contribution?". When constraints on action are loosened, employees are able to improvise more and come up with more autonomous initiatives. Thus, more emergent strategy is possible, making the Hoshin Planning Process also able to be effective in high velocity, high volatility and chaotic environments.

Knowing when you are using it

You can be sure your organisation is using this strategy execution process if "catchball" conversations are well known and occur at all levels of the organisations. "Catchball" conversations are one of the main ways breakthrough objectives are cascaded across all levels of the organisation. Other telltale signs include pervasiveness of Lean tools such as the A3 form, DMAIC, bowling charts and Kaizen events across all parts of the organisation.

Process strengths and shortcomings

There are five key strengths of Hoshin Planning. The first is the focus it brings to forming, cascading and implementing strategic objectives. The process does this by forcing strategic leaders to identify objectives that will deliver breakthrough results and then to prioritise three to five breakthrough objectives. In doing so, it ensures that all the possible strategic resources are squarely focused on the "vital few" or the critical objectives that matter most. This focus is deployed or cascaded across all levels of the organisation. Second, the Hoshin Planning Process forces widespread awareness of the strategy at every level of the organisation. Since it is cascaded at all levels of the organisation, every employee is involved in regular discussions of the strategy and progress towards that strategy. Third, the Hoshin Planning Process forces hands on leadership involvement at all levels. Catchball conversations are led by leaders at all levels. This makes it difficult for any leader to feign involvement or, worse, to sabotage the strategy by prioritising alternative projects. If this occurs, it will become visible quickly to others. The fourth strength of the Hoshin Planning Process is its ability to force alignment. Breakthrough objectives are cascaded down to every employee in the organisation. This makes it very difficult for departments, teams and individuals to pursue unaligned objectives without having first delivered on Hoshin Planning objectives deployed to them. Finally, the process forces clear ownership and accountability at all levels. So, if performance starts to fall short of expectations, the accountable people at all levels of the organisation will be visible. These five strengths of Hoshin Planning are not trivial, since absence of any of them is known to be one of the long-standing barriers to successful strategy implementation.

Like all processes, the Hoshin Planning Process also has some weaknesses. The first is its tendency to constrain most employee actions not aligned to the breakthrough objectives. While this has the benefits of focus, it simultaneously restricts employees from undertaking improvisatory actions and autonomous initiatives[13] that are not aligned to breakthrough objectives but that may be critical to the firm's future success and/or survival.[14] Consider, for example, the case of Intel, whose longevity and ability to thrive in a challenging industry has largely been driven by unintended but successful autonomous initiatives.[15] Second, the Hoshin Planning Process' annual strategy refresh rate may not be fast enough for some industries such as management consulting where the environment can change so much in a year that year-long strategies may be rendered obsolete within 6 months.[16] In high velocity and high volatility environments, strategic leaders may want to consider replacing annual objectives with quarterly objectives and 3–5-year objectives with annual objectives. A third weakness of the Hoshin Planning Process is that it requires significant leadership involvement at all levels of the organisation. In some organisations, effecting this level of involvement organisation-wide may be too much of a challenge. However, at a department or team level, it may be much easier. A fourth weakness of the Hoshin Planning Process is that it requires candour and the ability to constructively challenge each other in order to derive high-quality strategies. But in many organisations, people may see risks in speaking their minds and instead resort to creating political barriers to frustrate objectives they don't believe in. Finally, there is a risk of proliferation of targets and measures if strategic leaders do not ensure prioritisation and rationalisation of measures and targets. When this occurs, people may get overwhelmed and pay too much attention to the measures and targets that matter least over those that matter most.

Common tips and traps

To maximise success with this process, we recommend that the CEO invests a lot of time in ensuring top management team or dominant co-alition buy-in and ownership of the vision and breakthrough objectives. Further, top management team members should ensure that this level of buy-in and ownership is cascaded to all levels of the organisation. Doing so will go a long way to ensuring organisation-wide buy-in and engagement. When this doesn't occur, breakthrough objectives may be sidelined by operational requirements and unexpected crises of the moment. Therefore, the CEO and top management team need to avoid the trap of getting caught up in the operational demands of the moment at the expense of driving strategy realisation. We also recommend that the CEO and top management team avoid the trap of overreliance on measures and targets to drive strategy realisation. Instead, they should emphasise the spirit of the process by ensuring that essential activities such as strategy formation involvement, two-way "catchball" dialogue and support, ADRCA and progress review occur efficiently and effec-tively. Strategic leaders should also avoid the trap of relying on the re-fresh rate prescribed in the Hoshin Planning Process (i.e. 3–5-year plan and annual plan) as opposed to choosing the strategy refresh rate suited to their particular environment (e.g. quarterly breakthrough objectives and a monthly plan may be better for some environments). Finally, strategic leaders should avoid paying lip service to accountability for delivering on breakthrough objectives. We recommend they ensure ac-countability visibility at all levels and that incentives and disincentives are strongly aligned with this accountability. That is, they ensure that those who deliver are rewarded and those who do not are disincentive from not delivering in future.

Spotlight on the role of strategic leaders

Strong strategic leadership is fundamental to the functioning of the Hoshin Planning Process. This is because strong strategic leadership is essential to ensuring that the top management team or dominant coali-tion buy into the vision and breakthrough objectives; that they commit the necessary time for catchball dialogues and regular reviews; that they strike the right balance between forming SMART objectives and also objectives that allow the emergence of autonomous initiatives; that they encourage candour and remove political barriers to the process' func-tioning; and that they set a strategy refresh rate suited to the demands of the organisation's internal and external environment.

What if you are not a strategic leader?

If your organisation uses Hoshin Planning, then strategic objectives are cascaded from the top management team to every employee through catchball conversations. So, if you are not yet a strategic leader but want to maximise your contribution to your organisation's strategy, then these catchball conversations provide one of the best opportunities. During these sessions, you can get actively involved, ensure you speak with candour and constructively challenge proposed objectives to ensure your team decides to pursue the best quality ones. Outside of the sessions, you can maximise your contribution by doing everything in your power to deliver on the objectives, tasks and targets assigned to you. If you deliver these early, you can discuss with your line manager the different ways you could go above and beyond in contributing to the strategy. For example, you can support others to deliver on their objectives, tasks and targets so as to ensure your team is not the one that lets the organisation down by failing to deliver. On an ongoing basis, you can keep yourself current on how your organisation's environment is changing, what the emerging opportunities are for your organisation and what the risks are. In doing so, you will be in a stronger position to offer insightful suggestions during catchball sessions. You can also contribute by ensuring that you work efficiently and effectively so as to have free capacity to help your organisation should a crisis suddenly present itself. This way, will be able to help your organisation without compromising delivery of the objectives, tasks and targets you committed to. This is by no means an exhaustive list, but you can see how you can use catchball conversations to identify ways to contribute to the strategy beyond the objectives, tasks and targets allocated to you and to receive feedback on the impact of your additional efforts to contribute.

Notes

1   Ouda, H., & Ahmed, K. (2016). *A proposed systematic framework for applying Hoshin Kanri strategic planning methodology in educational institutions. European Scientific Journal, 12*(16), 158–194.
2   Pejsa, P., & Eng, R. (2011). Lean strategy deployment delivers customer satisfaction at GE Healthcare. *Global Business and Organizational Excellence, 30*(5), 45.
3   Pejsa, P., & Eng, R. (2011). Lean strategy deployment delivers customer satisfaction at GE Healthcare. *Global Business and Organizational Excellence, 30*(5), 45.
4   Pejsa, P., & Eng, R. (2011). Lean strategy deployment delivers customer satisfaction at GE Healthcare. *Global Business and Organizational Excellence, 30*(5), 45.

5 Johnson, C. N. (2002). The benefits of PDCA. *Quality Progress, 35*(5), 120.
6 Manos, A. (2007). The benefits of Kaizen and Kaizen events. *Quality Progress, 40*(2), 47.
7 Sokovic, M., Pavletic, D., & Pipan, K. K. (2010). Quality improvement methodologies – PDCA cycle, RADAR matrix, DMAIC and DFSS. *Journal of Achievements in Materials and Manufacturing Engineering, 43*(1), 476–483.
8 Schwagerman III, W. C., & Ulmer, J. M. (2013). The A3 lean management and leadership thought process. *Journal of Technology, Management & Applied Engineering, 29*(4), 1–10.
9 Pejsa, P., & Eng, R. (2011). Lean strategy deployment delivers customer satisfaction at GE Healthcare. *Global Business and Organizational Excellence, 30* (5), 45.
10 For example, see Kaplan, R. S., & Norton, D. P. (2008). *The execution premium: Linking strategy to operations for competitive advantage.* Boston, MA: Harvard Business School Publishing.
11 Anthony, J., & Banuelas, R. (2002). Key ingredients for the effective implementation of Six Sigma program. *Measuring Business Excellence, 6*(4), 20–27.
12 Husby, B., & Daniels, R. (2011). *Lean strategy deployment: Hoshin planning to align 13,000 staff.* Washington, DC: Alturam Institute.
13 Mirabeau, L., & Maguire, S. (2014). From autonomous strategic behavior to emergent strategy. *Strategic Management Journal, 35*, 1202–1229.
14 Burgelman, R. A. (1991). Intraorganizational ecology of strategy making and organizational adaptation: Theory and field research. *Organization Science, 2*(3), 239–262.
15 Burgelman, R. A., & Grove, A. S. (2007). Let chaos reign, then rein in chaos – repeatedly: Managing strategic dynamics for corporate longevity. *Strategic Management Journal, 28*(10), 964–979.
16 Busulwa, R. (2017). *The relationship between strategy execution and complexity* (PhD thesis). University of South Australia, Adelaide.

6 The Change Acceleration Process

Origin and design principles

Origin

The Change Acceleration Process was developed by Dr John Kotter, an emeritus professor of leadership at Harvard Business School, renowned thought leader on leading change, *New York Times* bestselling author on the topic and founder of the management consulting firm Kotter International. The process built on his research into change management. This research considered how leaders can best prepare and support their organizations to efficiently and effectively undertake organisational change. Through this research, Dr Kotter developed the well-known eight-step process for leading change. These eight steps included establishing a sense of urgency, creating a guiding coalition, developing a vision and strategy, communicating the change vision, empowering employees for broad-based action, generating short-term wins, consolidating gains to produce more change and, finally, anchoring the new approaches in the culture.

The eight-step Change Acceleration Process seems like an adaptation of Kotter's change leadership process, principles and insights to strategy execution. But Kotter argues that the 8 change "accelerators" differ from the eight-step change management methodology in three ways. First, they're concurrent and always at work as opposed to being episodic and sequential. Second, while the eight-step change management methodology is usually driven by a small powerful core team, the accelerators pull in as many people as possible throughout the organisation to form a "volunteer army". Finally, whereas the eight-step change management methodology is designed to work within a traditional hierarchy, the accelerators run on their own process built on a fluid, network-like structure.

The problem

In his research, Kotter observed that traditional organisation processes were designed for efficiency rather than strategic agility. Processes designed for efficiency emphasise control through hierarchical structures, policies and managerial routines. As such, these processes are best suited to delivering on the demands of day-to-day operations or predictable strategies in stable environments with minimal uncertainty. But such processes are not well suited for dynamic environments that require the ability to recognise and capitalise on fleeting opportunities or to dodge unexpected threats with speed and assurance. Yet Kotter's research revealed ample evidence of accelerating turbulence, volatility and disruption, making strategic agility critical. Thus, he sought to resolve a fundamental issue for organisations – how to deliver efficiency in day-to-day operations, while at the same time capitalising on fleeting opportunities and dodging threats. He proposed that to achieve both efficiency and strategic agility, organisations should run dual systems composed of the traditional hierarchy-based processes as well as the Change Acceleration Process.[1] In this way, the Change Acceleration Process can operate as an agile, network like structure designed to deliver strategic agility.

The idea in brief

The Change Acceleration Process is made up of eight steps or "Accelerators" that operate as network-like structure in parallel with the traditional hierarchy-based process. These accelerators are as follows: (1) create a sense of urgency around a single big opportunity, (2) build and maintain a guiding coalition (3) form the strategic vision and initiatives, (4) enlist a volunteer army, (5) enable action by removing barriers, (6) generate short-term wins, (7) sustain acceleration and, finally, (8) institute change. The eight accelerators are also guided by five principles that include having many change agents rather than the usual appointees; creating a "want to" and "get to" rather than "have to" mindset; engaging both head and heart, rather than just head; having more leadership rather than just management; and ensuring the Change Acceleration and the traditional hierarchy-based processes work as one rather than as silos (Figure 6.1).

Step 1: Create a sense of urgency around a big opportunity seeks to rid the organisation of complacency by focusing everyone's attention around a single strategically rational and emotionally exciting opportunity. This usually requires strategic leaders to do the groundwork to understand the complexity and volatility facing their

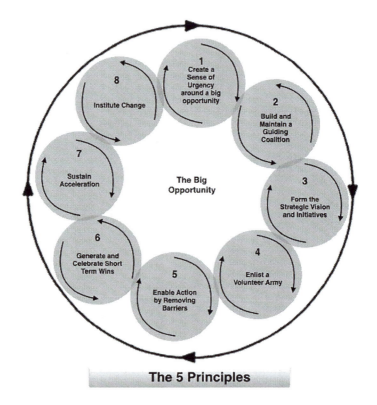

Figure 6.1 The Change Acceleration Process.

organisations and the time critical opportunities and threats facing the organisation. Having done so, they can identify the single most important opportunity that will transform the organisation's fortunes and the closing opportunity window within which to make it happen. Strategic leaders can then do what is necessary to ensure everyone in their organisation understands the importance of the opportunity and its urgency. Urgency starts at the top with the top management team. Thus, it is important that strategic leaders relentlessly communicate this urgency, model it through their behaviours, incentivise it and do everything else that is necessary for their people to wake up every morning determined to take better and faster action each day to move toward that opportunity.

Step 2: Build and maintain a guiding coalition seeks to assemble and maintain a team of people from all parts and all levels of the organisation who want to lead, be change agents and help others do the same in order to deliver on the big opportunity. Guiding coalition (GC) team members apply as volunteers for roles within the GC and are then selected for their skill sets and for the chance to represent each of the hierarchy's departments and levels. Kotter proposes that the GC must be made up of people from the leadership trust and must include some exceptional leaders and managers. In this way, the GC can be privy to important information to guide decisions about which initiatives to pursue and how to best pursue them. Kotter adds that all members of GC teams should be equal so that no hierarchical issues slow down the flow of information. While this may be uncomfortable for some team members at first, they usually come to enjoy it.

Step 3: Form the strategic vision and initiatives seeks to ensure creation of a vision to serve as a strategic true North for people in both the hierarchical process and the network-like process. Kotter proposes that an ideal vision is one that is easy to communicate, makes strategic sense, is easy to understand and is emotionally appealing. It should paint a picture of success and provide enough direction for the GC to be able to improvise and make decisions on the fly. Once a clear vision is established, the GC can go about identifying the key strategic initiatives it can work on to realise the vision. Kotter recommends that the GC should involve the top management team in the development of the strategic vision and initiatives in order to support alignment of the hierarchical and Change Acceleration Processes.

Step 4: Enlist a volunteer army seeks to ensure as many people as possible across the organisation want to help with a specific strategic initiative or with the vision in general. Kotter proposes that, as if by gravity, this volunteer army starts to pull the planets and moons into the work of the network-like process. A well-formed vision and strategic initiatives, communicated memorably and authentically by the GC, are often better received than communications from the hierarchy. Kotter proposes that such communication can go "viral", engaging, attracting and galvanising people across the whole organisation. The bigger and more galvanised the volunteer army, the more resources will be at the GC's disposal, the less resistance it will face and the faster it can realise the big opportunity.

Step 5: Enable action by removing barriers seeks to identify and swiftly remove any barriers that may emerge to slow or stop progress towards strategic initiatives or the vision. These barriers may be spotted by anyone across the organisation to reach the GC team or the volunteer army. On its reception, a member of the GC team or volunteer army may lead the rapid assembly of a "SWAT" team of different members of the volunteer army with the necessary resources and skills to snuff out the barrier so progress towards the strategic initiative or vision is no longer slowed down.

Step 6: Generate and celebrate short-term wins – In most organisations, the credibility of the Change Acceleration Process won't last long without early, clear and visible "wins" or benefits to the organisation. Cynics and sceptics may take the absence of such wins as evidence of the legitimacy of their doubts and may start to mount obstacles to thwart the Change Acceleration Process efforts. Thus, it is critical that the GC identifies, targets, delivers and publicly celebrates short-term wins. This can further galvanise the volunteer army and expand it. It can also shock the more sceptical parts of the organisation into paying attention to and respecting the work of the network-like structure. This is likely to lead to the eventual understanding and cooperation of more cynical managers and employees and, hence, accelerate realisation of the big opportunity.

Step 7: Sustain acceleration seeks to ensure that after delivering some significant wins, the GC does not fall into the temptation of slowing down, getting distracted or stopping. This would inevitably lead to dwindling of the volunteer army as they succumb to the "gravitational pull" of the hierarchical structure. To ensure this does not happen, the GC needs to find ways to refresh the vision and strategic initiatives in light of fleeting opportunities and threats, to sustain the sense of urgency, to continuously grow engagement and never take its foot off the gas.

Step 8: Institute change seeks to institutionalise wins into the hierarchy's processes, policies, routines and behaviours. It also seeks to legitimise and institute the Change Acceleration Process and the network-like structure into the organisation as if it were woven into the fabric of the organisation's DNA.

The five principles support the eight accelerators. The first principle, "having many change agents rather than the usual appointees", ensures an ever-expanding volunteer army to pursue the strategic initiatives and vision in an economically palatable way. The second principle, "creating a 'want to' and 'get to' rather than 'have to' mindset", is aimed at tapping into the spirit of volunteerism and the desire to voluntarily work with others for a shared purpose. This provides the opportunity to mobilise more and more of the organisation's extensive brain power and energy. The third principle, "engaging both head and heart rather than just head", is aimed at appealing to people's emotions too rather than just to logic. Since volunteers are essentially being asked to have a day job in the hierarchical structure and a night job in the network-like structure, they must have compelling head and heart reasons to do this. The fourth principle, "having much more leadership rather than just management", acknowledges that the network-like structure is largely driven by inspirational leadership rather than management. While some management functions are still essential, much more leadership is needed. Finally, the fifth principle, "ensuring the Change Acceleration and the traditional hierarchy-based processes work as one rather than as silos", points to the dual importance of the traditional hierarchy for efficiently delivering day-to-day operational processes and the network-like structure for delivering the strategic agility necessary for the organisation to survive and thrive. The two are both essential and inseparable, and thus one cannot be compromised at the expense of the other; for example, the network-like structure is essentially resourced by the hierarchical structure, but the hierarchical structure's sustainable survival depends on the success of the network-like structure. The two also can't operate in silos, since information, decisions and changes need to flow between them for both to work efficiently and effectively.

Caveats

The Change Acceleration Process steps or accelerators are not episodic and sequential but always at work, even if aspects of some may have to start before others. Also, as previously discussed, while the Change Acceleration Process has many similarities to Kotter's eight-step change management methodology, there are some key differences. While the change management methodology is usually driven by a small powerful core, the accelerators pull in as many people as possible throughout the organisation to form a "volunteer army". Further, whereas the eight-step change management methodology is designed to work within a traditional hierarchy, the accelerators run alongside it but on their own process built on a fluid, network-like structure.

What you might know it as

If you're familiar with Kotter's work on change management, and in particular his eight-step change management model, you will find the Change Acceleration Process very similar, albeit with the caveats about the differences discussed earlier. You may also find the setup of the network-like structure supporting the Change Acceleration Process similar to the setup of project organisation structures. There are, of course, some fundamental differences. These are largely encapsulated in the five principles underpinning the Change Acceleration Process. But also, project organisation structures and processes tend to be more episodic and to rely more on hierarchical governance approaches, whereas the network-like structure process is more iterative and relies more on inspirational leadership of volunteers. If you have worked in a matrix organisation structure before, you may find some of the dual structure approaches to pursuing strategic initiatives familiar.

Prevalence

Across all sectors, we found 12 per cent of organisations, or about 1 in every 10 organisations, using the Change Acceleration Process to some degree to execute strategy. But this usage rate comes with a caveat – many study participants confused use of the Change Acceleration Process with of change management methodology to execute strategy. The Change Acceleration Process is relatively new, having emerged in the popular literature between 2012 and 2014. That being said, if those citing use of change management methods for strategy execution are taken as likely users of the Change Acceleration Process, users of the Change Acceleration Process are likely to be 1 in 10 across all sectors except NGO/NFP organisations, which show greater use of the process. Change management was associated with high to very high execution effectiveness in obvious environments and in complex but low volatility environments. But because of participant confusion of the Change Acceleration Process with the change management process, the effectiveness of the Change Acceleration Process in different environments was not clear (see Figure 6.2).

Process	Sector				Employees (Org Size)				
	Public Sector / Government	Private Sector	NGO/NFP	All Sectors	>500	51-499	2 - 50	<2	All Sizes
7 Factor Process	10%	13%	25%	13%	19%	10%	10%	0%	12%
Execution Premium Process	24%	16%	25%	18%	25%	21%	13%	11%	18%
Simple Rules	14%	20%	17%	18%	13%	21%	23%	44%	21%
Lean Strategy Deployment Process	14%	19%	25%	18%	22%	21%	15%	11%	18%
Change Acceleration Process	14%	11%	17%	12%	9%	21%	10%	11%	12%
Project Management Process	53%	80%	66%	70%	88%	84%	63%	33%	72%
Talent Placement Process	14%	27%	25%	23%	22%	26%	23%	11%	22%
Outcomes and Incentives / Disincentives Communication Process	24%	28%	25%	26%	31%	26%	25%	11%	26%
Learning on the Run Process	39%	38%	50%	38%	31%	42%	43%	22%	37%
Resource Allocation / Portfolio Management Process	19%	17%	25%	18%	22%	21%	18%	66%	24%
Performance Monitoring and Feedback Process	39%	38%	50%	38%	44%	37%	43%	0%	38%

Figure 6.2 Proportion of study participants citing use of the Change Acceleration Process by sector and organisation size.★

Note: ★For example, of the 241 study participants, 50 participants were from the public sector/government. Of these 50 public sector/government participants, 5 participants (10%) used the 7 Factor Process. This table differs from Tables 6.23 and 6.24 shown in Busulwa (2016), where process users in each sector are shown as a proportion of all study participants. So, in the case of public sector/government, users of the 7 Factor Process is shown as 2% (i.e. 5/241 = 2%).

The process in action

To demonstrate the process in action, we use a case drawn from Kotter's book on the Change Acceleration Process. The case study tracks the adoption, implementation and use of the Change Acceleration Process by the field sales division of a large organisation to execute strategy. As you read the case, pay attention to how the division approaches each step of the Change Acceleration Process as well as how it carries out the activities within that step and the tools it uses to carry out the different steps and activities. Also consider the organisation's unique context, the challenges of this context for the Change Acceleration Process and how the organisation overcomes these challenges to realise the benefits of using this particular process. As you review the case, if you believe the Change Acceleration Process suits your organisation's unique context, you may be able to adapt some of the approaches in the case study to your organisation's approach to the process. Alternatively, you may decide that the process is not suited to your particular organisation – in which case one or more of the other processes in this book may be more suitable. Still, there may be particular strategy execution insights and practices that you can pick up and adapt to whatever process you are using. For example, the steps and activities on creating a sense of urgency and generating quick wins are likely to be valuable practices to adapt to any strategy execution process.

Case study: Davidson's field sales organisation: seizing an opportunity to become the best sales organisation in the industry[2]

Paul Davidson led a team of sales executives from the division of a B2B technology company. Paul had noticed a concerning sales decline over the last 2 years. He commissioned a consultancy firm to undertake a review which he could in turn discuss with his division head and the company CEO. The consultancy firm found that not only had market share declined, but that Davidson's firm had slid into fifth place in the industry. The consultants made additional findings, including that Davidson's firm lagged behind competitors in setting up operations in Asia; that Davidson's firm had higher per unit sales costs relative to industry leaders; that customers were making more purchases through intermediaries; and that industry leaders had caught onto this trend and adapted their sales approach but Davidson's organisation had not.

Davidson discussed the consultant's findings and possible initiatives to address them with his division head and with the CEO. He gained their support but received no additional resources with which to carry out the initiatives.

Having come across the Change Acceleration Process, Paul Davidson set out to utilise it in parallel with his organisation's existing processes. He began Step 1 by convening a meeting of the sales division's executive committee. He laid out the findings from the consultants and their implications. He also pointed out that there was zero chance of new people being hired to carry out any strategic initiatives and that the sales division needed to find a way to get more out of its current people. Davidson charged the team with coming up with a statement spelling out the big opportunity for the organisation. The statement had to be positive, short, clear and energising, with no gloom, threats or consequences. It also had to be set up in such a way that change resisters and analytical people wouldn't shoot it down. Further, the statement had to be something that the executive committee itself deeply believed in and was inspired by. Over the course of the whole day and through carefully facilitated small and large group exercises, the team came up with the following statement:

> *We're convinced we have an opportunity to increase our sales growth significantly in two years, and to become the best sales organisation in the industry. This is a realistic because (1) customer needs are changing, requiring competitors to change, but it is not certain they can change fast enough; (2) markets in developing economies are starting to grow explosively; and (3) we are clearly not operating at peak efficiency within the company. We have not changed fast enough to keep up with external demands, even though we have excellent people. We're capable of changing faster — we've done it in the past when we were smaller. If we handle this right, there is no reason why we cannot create an exceptionally successful field organisation of which everyone — starting with us — will be deeply proud to be a part.*

At the end of the daylong meeting, one of Davidson's staff volunteered to put together a volunteer team that could continue what had been started that day. Davidson insisted that the team not be a typical task force. It came to eventually be made up of

21 volunteers from across the field organisation globally. Coming from across the hierarchy and across the sales value chain, the team had broad capability and credibility. Their mandate was to create urgency and get faster change embraced intellectually and emotionally around their "Big Opportunity" statement. They agreed on an ambitious goal: to get a minimum of half of the 4,000-member sales organisation to sincerely support the statement and start behaving accordingly. The team spent 4 months devising and implementing ideas to catalyse a broad understanding of, passion for, and commitment to the ideas in the Big Opportunity statement. They held team teleconferences every 2 weeks and organised into subgroups to undertake specific initiatives. The "urgency team" and its subgroups were creative, resourceful and relentless in pursuit of their objectives. Activities undertaken to communicate the vision, create buy-in and attract a growing volunteer army included developing and providing line managers with support materials to engage their groups, videos, blogs, success stories and speaking spots at standardised meetings that brought together large numbers of people from the sales organisation. For example, at the annual sales management meeting, they were able to get organisers to give them a quarter of the agenda to devote to the Big Opportunity. In these appearances, the urgency team used their most credible and engaging members to communicate the vision and create buy-in.

Just as the urgency team was about to achieve its ambitious goal, Davidson sent out an email inviting employees to apply for a 1-year role as part of a new kind of organisation he was building called the Guiding Coalition. He explained that the purpose of the Coalition would be to attract and help guide the volunteers who would accelerate capitalising on the Big Opportunity. Applicants had to outline why they wanted to be part of the Coalition, how they planned to manage the additional workload and the ideas they had to take advantage of the Big Opportunity. A subgroup of the urgency team selected 35 people from the 210 applicants, ensuring broad representation geographically, across the hierarchy and across the sales value chain. This was in addition to applicants having compelling applications, having strong credibility and the right motivations. The sales executive committee then signed off on the final team of 35. Davidson sent a note to the selected applicants to notify them of their selection, why they had been selected and their mandate. He also sent a note to those who hadn't been selected outlining why and how their leadership was still needed to achieve the Big Opportunity. The Coalition began with a 2-day offsite for team building and to work out how the team would function to be more of a meritocracy with the people having the best information, connections, motivation and skills, taking the lead on relevant initiatives.

With input from volunteers, colleagues throughout the organisation, the consultants' report and the executives' Big Opportunity statement, the Coalition assembled a change vision statement of what it would achieve in the next 12 months. They ran it past the sales executive committee who were pleasantly surprised by its boldness. Once this change vision was established, the Coalition translated it into specific initiatives and ran these past the sales executive committee. They discussed alignment and how to best support the Coalition's efforts without negatively disrupting existing operating plans and projects. Initially, the relationship between the sales executive committee members and the Coalition struggled and Davidson had to seek external consultant support for its proper functioning. With coaching from the external consultant, Davidson began to model essential behaviours for the sales executive committee to support the Coalition by cheering them on, helping them overcome obstacles and treating them as a partner rather than just another task force. The Coalition amplified and extended the urgency team's earlier methods to attract volunteers and drive implementation of the initiatives. They found that much of their work was about finding and removing barriers that prevented volunteers from carrying out activities in support of the initiatives and resolving territorial issues between the Coalition's efforts and existing organisation efforts. The Coalition began to build a track record of small and significant wins which were continuously celebrated by the sales executive committee each time. This boosted the Coalition's credibility and resulted in a growing number of volunteers and even more momentum. Mistakes and issues occurred along the way, but the Coalition was quick to resolve these before they could sap engagement and morale. They persisted, kept learning and improving until after 2 years, the team and their way of doing things were accepted and appreciated by the whole sales organisation. Over the 2-year period, Davidson's field organisation grew sales by 44 per cent, winning back market share to move to the number two position in its industry. Its market capitalisation also grew by 155 per cent.

Are you in the right environment for this process?

The data showed the change management process to be highly effective in obvious and complex but low volatility environments. Unfortunately, due study participant confusion between change management and change acceleration, there was no clear evidence of which environments the Change Acceleration Process was most effective in. Kotter proposes that it is a process for achieving strategic agility. Such processes are usually designed for flexibility to respond to unexpected threats and opportunities as well as to encourage the emergence of autonomous strategic initiatives. Depending on how tightly the GC defines and controls discretionary efforts in the pursuit of strategic initiatives, the process may or may not enable realisation of emergent strategy or flexibility to adapt to disruption. However, operating as part of a dual structure, there is a clear vehicle for the realisation of deliberate strategic initiatives. These can be realised either as strategic initiatives executed by the GC or as strategic initiatives executed by the hierarchical structure. To the extent that it encourages the emergence of autonomous strategic initiatives and realisation of emergent strategy, the dual structure nature of the Change Acceleration Process makes it suitable for use in all environments. Its effectiveness in all environments will then depend on the extent to which the organisation's resources are deployed to the hierarchical structure versus the network-like structure. For instance, in a highly chaotic and volatile environment, the majority of resources may be better deployed to the network-like structure, whereas in a more stable environment the majority of resources may be better deployed to the hierarchical structure.

Knowing when you are using it

You are likely to be using the Change Acceleration Process if the eight steps or accelerators described earlier resemble one way your organisation executes strategy and this process is in addition to a more traditional hierarchical process. Other telltale indicators include the existence of a GC-like team and calls for volunteers to fill roles within the GC-like team or within a volunteer team working on key strategic initiatives.

Process strengths and shortcomings

A key strength of the Change Acceleration Process includes its ability to drive out complacency within the organisation. In pursuing the creation of a sense of urgency, it focuses employee's attention on the organisation's threats and opportunities and makes a strategically rational and emotionally exciting case to be motivated and take action. Second, by operating the Change Acceleration Process' network-like structure in parallel with the organisation's existing hierarchical process that is geared for efficiency, the Change Acceleration Process can enable an organisation to be ambidextrous. The caveat, as we've pointed out earlier, is that the GC encourages the emergence and pursuit of autonomous strategic initiatives. If it constrains such initiatives, then its ability to create ambidexterity is diminished. When this happens, its ability to help the organisation adapt is diminished, since emergent strategy realisation is essential to adaptation. The Change Acceleration Process' reliance on volunteers to get things done can also be a strength, insofar as it is able to tap into employee's capabilities beyond the defined job boundaries of the hierarchical structure. This reliance on volunteers can also be an important barometer of organisation morale, since it is likely that there is a positive association between morale levels and the number of applicants to join the GC or the volunteer army.

Potential weaknesses of the Change Acceleration Process include its reliance on volunteers either having unutilised capacity or being able to work in the hierarchical structure during business hours and in the network-like structure outside of business hours. In some organisations, both the unutilised capacity and the ability to work in the network-like structure outside of business hours may be a challenge to tap into. Another potential weakness of the Change Acceleration Process is that the literature on it and prescriptions on how to use it do not discuss how to drive the realisation of emergent strategy. In not doing this, it can come across as a parallel process to the hierarchical structure for accelerating the delivery of important deliberate strategic initiatives. This would of course benefit the organisation in seizing deliberate opportunities faster and better adapting to crises. But the organisation would still be missing out on the benefits of autonomous strategic initiatives. Finally, it is possible that users of this process may underestimate the gravitational pull of the hierarchical structure, resulting in tensions between the hierarchical structure leaders and the network-like structure leaders. We anticipate that for it to work effectively, the GC ought to have equally strong leaders from the top management team within its membership and incentives that align to the dual approach. That is, although everyone in the GC may be equal, some GC members may be more equal than others in overcoming the gravitational pull of the hierarchical structure.

Common tips and traps

To get the best out of this process, we recommend that users pay particular attention to adhering to the principles underpinning the process. If users of the process fall into the trap of circumventing the principles, the process may come across like just another extension of the hierarchical structure, and it may fail to attract sufficient volunteers or to effectively keep them engaged. We also recommend that users pay particular attention to how they can enable the pursuit of emergent strategies within the Change Acceleration Process. If users fall into the trap of only pursuing deliberate strategies, they may miss out on a once-in-a-lifetime, unintended opportunities. For example, much of Intel's survival and strength today can be attributed to such emergent strategic opportunities. Further, incentives may be necessary to help maintain the balance between day-to-day and off-hours activity. Without these incentives, the "gravitational pull" is usually back to operational activity in the long run.

Spotlight on the role of strategic leaders

As with all processes, the importance of strong strategic leadership can often be underestimated. Thus, we recommend that the top management team consider assigning the crown jewels (i.e. the best of the best) of its leadership trust to the network-like structure. This will be fundamental in establishing the network-like structure and to initially sustaining its legitimacy. Strong strategic leadership is essential to ensuring that the top management team or dominant coalition buys into the vision and strategic initiatives, that they commit to supporting the network-like structure and to giving volunteers within their teams' permission to work in the network-like structure. They also need to model the right attitudes and behaviours for their teams and to assist the GC to remove political barriers to the process' functioning. Further, strategic leaders need to play an important role in ensuring teams within both the hierarchical structure and the network-like structure recognise their interdependence and work to support each other. Without this, rather than better positioning the organisation, the opposite may occur by the work of both being derailed by infighting and covert politics.

What if you are not a strategic leader?

If you are not a strategic leader, this process can provide you with almost as much opportunity as a strategic leader to contribute to the strategy. First, you can contribute by ensuring you deliver or over-deliver in your job within the hierarchical structure. By continuing to deliver or over-deliver in the hierarchical structure, you may be provided with free time to volunteer in the network-like structure during business hours. Outside business hours, you have much more opportunity to contribute to strategic initiatives of the network-like structure. You can volunteer for particular roles within the GC or the volunteer army. You can join as many projects as you want to within the network-like structure. Once you prove your value and ability to over-deliver in the network structure as well, you are likely to be sought out to join a range of teams working on different issues. If you are unsure how to contribute to the network-like structure initially, you can seek advice from members of the GC regarding the different ways you can maximise your contribution to the organisation's strategy. But it is important to keep in mind that you can't use your involvement in the network-like structure as an excuse to under-deliver in your role within the hierarchical structure. Doing so may drive your line manager to seek to constrain your involvement in the network-like structure both within business hours and outside of business hours. Another approach you can take is to seek your line manager's and strategic leaders' advice on how to maximise your contribution to the network-like structure.

Notes

1 Kotter, J. (2012). Accelerate! *Harvard Business Review*, November.
2 Adapted from Kotter, J. P. (2014). *Accelerate: Building strategic agility for a faster-moving world.* , Boston, MA: Harvard Business School Publishing.

7 The Resource Allocation Process

Origin and design principles

Origin

The Resource Allocation Process is built on the premise that strategy execution is achieved by a series of resource commitments. This process emerged out of a synthesis of decades-long research into resource allocation, predominantly by Joseph Bower, and the strategy execution activities identified by participants in our study. Joseph Bower is a professor of Business Administration at Harvard Business School and has been a seminal general management thought leader for more than 51 years. His original work challenged the view that an organisation's strategy is either consciously deliberated by top management or carefully crafted by strategy and planning staff through sophisticated analysis.[1] Instead, his research revealed that an organisation's realised strategy was usually the result of the many day-to-day decisions made by managers at all levels of the organisation about the resources to commit to policies, programs, people and facilities.[2] He proposed that this was due to the unavoidable realities in organisational life such as politics, competing interests, differences in access to information, differences in access to resources and limitations on management control. These realities limited the ability of top managers to form, push down and command the realisation of strategies. For example, not having technical knowledge of front-line staff, of products, of customers and of markets may result in top management forming unrealisable strategies. While strategic initiatives formed by front-line and middle managers with this technical, staff, customer and market knowledge were more likely to be realised, they were impeded by issues such as insufficient resources, lack of management attention and key stakeholder barriers.

Noticing these issues, Bower proposed the Resource Allocation Process as an approach for organisations to realise strategy by having the bottom-up initiatives of front-line and middle managers compete for scarce corporate resources and top management attention in order to survive and make it through to realisation. Over time, a number of highly regarded management thinkers added to and extended the Resource Allocation Process, including Stanford Professor of Management and Academy of Management Fellow Robert Burgelman; Harvard Professor of Management and Innosight co-founder Clayton Christensen; Harvard Professor of Management and Brigham Young University President Clark Gilbert; Harvard Business School researcher and Shizenkan University founder Tomo Noda; London Business School Management Professor and former management consultant Donald Sull; and Harvard Management Professor and Rock Centre for Entrepreneurship and Harvard MBA Program Chair Thomas Eisenmann.

The problem

Having established that realised strategy was usually not the result of consciously deliberated top-down strategies, resource allocation researchers then sought to investigate whether top managers could actually influence this bottom-up process and, if so, what activities they could engage in to influence it in such a way as to optimise strategy realisation. This was a fundamental and unaddressed problem that was eventually resolved incrementally. Over time, researchers resolved it by identifying a range of levers top managers could use to influence the Resource Allocation Process, including shaping the structural context,[3] shaping the strategic context,[4] mediating the influence of powerful capital providers[5] and powerful customers,[6] making and effecting resource allocation decisions,[7] making and effecting resource withdrawal decisions[8] and having appropriate capabilities and infrastructure.[9]

The idea in brief

The key steps in the Resource Allocation Process are as follows: (1) clarify strategic priorities for every part of the organisation, (2) allocate or withdraw top-down initiatives resources as necessary, (3) encourage the emergence of bottom-up initiatives, (4) identify and nurture bottom-up initiatives, (5) allocate or withdraw bottom-up initiatives resources as necessary, (6) create a way for leaders to circumvent the regular Resource Allocation Process, (7) shepherd initiative leaders from powerful stakeholders who may derail them, and (8) be vigilant and intervene to resolve conflicts, fight inertia and accelerate delivery of critical initiatives. What follows is the unpacking and justification of each step based on the findings of Resource Allocation Process researchers as well as the findings from our field interviews and questionnaire surveys with executive, middle management and front-line employees (Figure 7.1).

Step 1: Clarify strategic priorities and provide enabling structures, capabilities and tools requires top managers to perform two critical roles to set their organisations up for optimal use of the Resource Allocation Process. The first is to outline a clear and compelling strategic direction for the organisation, with equally clear and compelling strategic priorities for the short, medium and long term.[10] Similar to other strategy execution processes, this will usually require top managers to do the ongoing groundwork of understanding and keeping their finger on the pulse of changes within their internal and external environment, that is, the implications for their organisation, the time critical opportunities and threats facing their organisation and therefore the critical strategic priorities in the short, medium and long

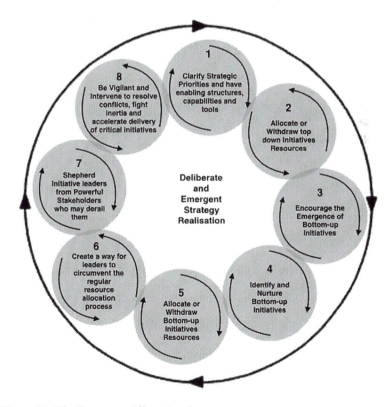

Figure 7.1 The Resource Allocation Process.

term. They then need to ensure that everyone in their organisation understands the threats and opportunities and buys into the organisation's vision and strategic priorities. For example, this may require top managers to relentlessly communicate the strategic direction and its rationale, to model its importance through their behaviours and actions, to incentivise contribution to it and to do everything else that is necessary for their people to wake up every morning determined to take better and faster action in their day to move towards the vision and strategic priorities. Having done the first part, the second part requires top managers to provide the enabling structures, capabilities and tools to support use of the Resource Allocation Process.[11] It may be that the organisation's existing structures, capabilities and tools are configured to support a traditional historical budgeting process, for example. If this is the case, they may need to be reconfigured to be able to also support the Resource Allocation Process. Measurement and reporting systems, incentive and disincentive systems and other organisational and administrative mechanisms may also need to be reconfigured to encourage and accelerate the formation and realisation of bottom-up initiatives.[12]

Step 2: Allocate or withdraw top-down initiatives resources – Most organisations using the Resource Allocation Process will usually have an already established top-down Resource Allocation Process. This top-down process may, for example, have important operations improvement initiatives such as quality or efficiency improvement initiatives. But it may also have high priority strategic initiatives being pushed organisation-wide by the top management team. Some of these initiatives may have initially been bottom-up initiatives that are now being scaled for exploitation. In either case, as resources are scarce in organisations, the allocation of resources to new or high priority strategic initiatives will often require ongoing review of what resources need to remain allocated to top-down initiatives, what resources need to be increased and what resources need to be redeployed from other initiatives that are of lower priority.

Step 3: Encourage the emergence of bottom-up initiatives seeks to ensure that people at all levels of the organisation understand the organisation mandate for bottom-up initiatives. That is, they need to be clear that the future of the organisation may depend on one or more or a combination of the bottom-up initiatives being formed by people. Once they understand this, they then need to understand the organisation genuinely wants them to form bottom-up initiatives, that it is shaping the environment for their creation and that it is providing employees with opportunities to form and pursue bottom-up initiatives. Employees then need to see that the formation and pursuit of bottom-up initiatives is authorised, invested in, celebrated and rewarded on an ongoing basis. Such efforts are examples of the many approaches that can be taken to encourage the emergence of bottom-up initiatives. The better the approach, the better the number and quality of bottom-up initiatives that will emerge.

Step 4: Identify and nurture bottom-up initiatives – Issues such as differences in access to information, differences in access to resources and differences in ability may stifle some bottom-up initiatives. Such initiatives may be rough diamonds, with their originators perhaps lacking the skills to pitch their value or lacking the necessary know-how or resources to develop them to a point where their commercial value is apparent. Because of issues such as these, strategic leaders need to be continuously monitoring, spotting and nurturing nascent initiatives to ensure these are developed to a point where their viability can be properly evaluated. If this does not occur, many a rough diamond may be starved of resources and die off before they develop to a level where people see the real potential. For instance, in the 1970s, Xerox's subsidiary Xerox Parc developed many of the foundational technologies we depend on today such as laser printing, Ethernet, the modern personal computer, graphical user interfaces and ubiquitous computing. But its strategic leaders did not identify or nurture these initiatives to a point where their commercial potential could be realised and exploited. Instead, entrepreneurs such as Steve Jobs and Bill Gates, who were fortunate enough to visit Xerox Parc and see these nascent product initiatives,[13] nurtured and transformed those product initiatives into global businesses that not only dwarf the size of Xerox today but are likely to outlive it. Strategic leaders can nurture strategic initiatives in numerous ways, including providing seed resources to further develop them, becoming active sponsors of initiative leaders and using their contacts to get initial customers.

Step 5: Allocate or withdraw bottom-up initiatives resources – Similar to Step 2, this step requires top managers to undertake ongoing review of what resources need to remain allocated to existing bottom-up initiatives, what resources allocated to existing bottom-up initiatives need to be increased, what resources to existing bottom-up initiatives need to be withdrawn and what resources need to be allocated to new bottom-up initiatives. Joseph Bower and Clark Gilbert recommend that strategic leaders get to understand the people proposing, leading and backing bottom-up initiatives and their judgement track record over time. This can be a much more valuable indicator of potential than sophisticated number crunching. In some situations, this step may involve strategic leaders dramatically ramping up their investments in bottom-up strategic initiatives and shifting them to the top-down initiative group for company-wide exploitation. For example, in 2003, Intel Corporation allocated hundreds of millions of dollars to developing infrastructure for the Centrino processor and then hundreds of millions of dollars to market it. This was a dramatic reallocation of resources to what was once a bottom-up initiative provided with minimal resources and top management attention. The initiative was then also shifted into the top-down Resource Allocation Process so that it could be fully scaled and exploited as a core product of the organisation.

Step 6: Create a way for leaders to circumvent the regular Resource Allocation Process – Truly disruptive ideas can at first seem absurd and are therefore likely to get sidelined by the top-down Resource Allocation Process. Originators of such ideas may have to work in stealth mode to not be perceived as persona non grata within the organisation or within their teams. Top managers can build opportunities for these "rebels" to circumvent regular processes in order to further develop their ideas until the commercial potential can be known. Examples of such opportunities might include creation of spin-out units, joint venture projects, related acquisitions, experimental projects and sabbaticals. Other examples can include public support for these rebels to increase their credibility and thus their potential to receive cooperation from others in the organisation.

Step 7: Shepherd initiative leaders from powerful stakeholders who may derail them – It is a reality of organisational life that powerful resource providers, powerful customers and other powerful stakeholders may inadvertently or deliberately use their power to derail nascent bottom-up initiatives. Thus, top managers need to be vigilant to the effect of these powerful stakeholders on emerging bottom-up initiatives and use top management's power to shepherd initiative leaders, so that their initiatives can be developed to a point where the commercial potential can be properly evaluated. An example of this is former General Electric CEO Jack Welch's practice of looking for such leaders and throwing his power behind them to protect them and their projects from their line managers and their manager's managers. Jack Welch would provide his direct line to such initiative leaders and ask them to call him if anyone got in their way. He would also make this clear to their various levels of managers. Top managers in every organisation will have their own approach, but the point is to be alert to the power and political barriers initiative leaders face and go to bat for them if necessary. The nascent bottom-up initiative saved may be one that eventually changes the fortunes of the entire organisation.

Step 8: Be vigilant and intervene to resolve conflicts, fight inertia and accelerate delivery of critical initiatives – A range of competing interests exist in organisations that can stifle the emergence of bottom-up initiatives. Such competing interests can arise from issues such as crossing territorial boundaries, having to share or lose key resources, not receiving credit or being discredited and many more. Without intervention, these issues can fester and dramatically slow down the emergence of bottom-up initiatives or the quality of such initiatives. Thus, this step requires top managers to be vigilant to these issues and to intervene to put the organisation's interests ahead of competing interests to accelerate the formation and realisation of critical initiatives.

Caveats

As with other strategy execution processes, the Resource Allocation Process steps are not episodic and sequential but always at work, even if aspects of some may have to start before others. Many strategy execution processes discuss or imply the need for resource allocation for the realisation of strategies. Some processes have explicit stages for this. For instance, the 7 Factor Process' Step 3 is "Allocate financial, time and talent resources for implementation". And the Execution Premium Process prescribes the authorisation and protection of funding for strategic initiatives. The Resource Allocation Process differs from these other processes in that it focuses on configuring resource allocation to drive strategy realisation. The Resource Allocation Process does not advocate removal of traditional budgeting processes, which may be instrumental to maintaining existing value delivery. Researches also do not suggest that the Resource Allocation Process needs to be run in isolation; that is, it can be run in parallel with other processes which may deliver different benefits in parallel to those delivered by the Resource Allocation Process. However, the process does imply the need to maintain a suitable level of uncommitted resources to judiciously allocate to new or successful bottom-up initiatives whenever such initiatives emerge. The ultimate success of the Resource Allocation Process depends on employees wanting to and being able to invest their efforts into forming new initiatives, on middle managers and/or senior managers nurturing these initiatives to a point where their commercial potential can be determined with confidence and on top managers making appropriate and timely investment and disinvestment decisions.

What you might know it as

As discussed earlier, most strategy execution processes explicitly or implicitly require some form of resource allocation, since strategy execution is usually a resource-consuming activity. So, it's possible you may know the Resource Allocation Process as elements of other strategy execution processes. Most of these other strategy execution processes discuss the importance of resource allocation for strategy execution but are limited in their guidance on how to do it. If you are familiar with contemporary management accounting and finance practices or literatures, aspects of the Resource Allocation Process may be familiar to you. Such practices and literature may discuss linking budgeting and strategy processes, for example. If you are familiar with project management or quality improvement literatures, you may find discussions of the need for specific project or initiative resources separate to the operating budget being needed.

Prevalence

Across all sectors, we found 18 per cent of organisations, or one in every five organisations, using the Resource Allocation Process to execute strategy. Unlike other processes where usage varied across sectors and organisation sizes, usage of the Resource Allocation Process was about the same across sectors and organisation sizes. The Resource Allocation Process was mostly associated with high execution effectiveness in obvious environments. Across all environments, more than half of organisations making extensive use of this process cited execution effectiveness above peers (see Figure 7.2).

| | Sector | | | | Employees (Org Size) | | | | |
Process	Public Sector / Government	Private Sector	NGO/NFP	All Sectors	>500	51-499	2 - 50	<2	All Sizes
7 Factor Process	10%	13%	25%	13%	19%	10%	10%	0%	12%
Execution Premium Process	24%	16%	25%	18%	25%	21%	13%	11%	18%
Simple Rules	14%	20%	17%	18%	13%	21%	23%	44%	21%
Lean Strategy Deployment Process	14%	19%	25%	18%	22%	21%	15%	11%	18%
Change Acceleration Process	14%	11%	17%	12%	9%	21%	10%	11%	12%
Project Management Process	53%	80%	66%	70%	88%	84%	63%	33%	72%
Talent Placement Process	14%	27%	25%	23%	22%	26%	23%	11%	22%
Outcomes and Incentives / Disincentives Communication Process	24%	28%	25%	26%	31%	26%	25%	11%	26%
Learning on the Run Process	39%	38%	50%	38%	31%	42%	43%	22%	37%
Resource Allocation / Portfolio Management Process	19%	17%	25%	18%	22%	21%	18%	66%	24%
Performance Monitoring and Feedback Process	39%	38%	50%	38%	44%	37%	43%	0%	38%

Figure 7.2 Proportion of study participants citing use of the Resource Allocation Process by sector and organisation size.★

Note: ★For example, of the 241 study participants, 50 participants were from the public sector/government. Of these 50 public sector/government participants, 5 participants (10%) used the 7 Factor Process. This table differs from Tables 6.23 and 6.24 shown in Busulwa (2016), where process users in each sector are shown as a proportion of all study participants. So, in the case of public sector/government users of the 7 Factor Process, this is shown as 2% (i.e. 5/241 = 2%).

The process in action

To demonstrate the Resource Allocation Process in action, we use the case study of a large telecommunications organisation's use of the Resource Allocation process in parallel with its traditional financial management processes. To avoid potential confusion, we restrict our focus on a single bottom-up initiative. In reality, organisations will likely have many bottom-up and top-down initiatives in flight at a given time. As you read the case, pay attention to how the organisation approaches each step of the Resource Allocation Process as well as how it carries out the activities within that step. Also consider the organisation's unique setting, the challenges of this context for the Resource Allocation Process and how the organisation overcomes these challenges to realise the benefits of using the Resource Allocation Process. As you review the case, if you believe the Resource Allocation Process suits your organisation's unique setting, you may be able to adapt some of the approaches in the case study to form your organisation's unique approach to the process. Alternatively, you may decide that the process is not suited to your particular organisation – in which case one or more of the other processes in this book, or a combination of them, may be more suitable. As with other processes you may have already explored, there may be particular strategy execution insights and practices that you can pick up and adapt to whatever approach you choose to take to strategy execution.

Case study: using the Resource Allocation Process at a large telecommunications organisation: BellSouth's bottom-up mobile phone opportunity[14]

BellSouth Corporation (today known as BellSouth LLC) was one of seven operating companies formed in 1984 when the US Department of Justice forced AT&T to divest itself of its regional companies. At the time of its formation, it had operating revenue of $10.7 billion, net income of $1.4 billion and net assets of $21.4 billion. The creation of BellSouth brought together the companies providing telephone services in the south-eastern United States. In this case study, we track the journey of a single bottom-up initiative through the BellSouth Resource Allocation Process. The initiative is cellular telephone services, also referred to as wireless or mobile telephone services. At the time of BellSouth's formation, nascent mobile telephone services were a novelty for most Americans and the company's managers were uncertain of the future commercial potential of such technologies. BellSouth inherited a business plan from AT&T, which outlined clear strategic priorities for each business unit and product line. These targets were translated into short, medium and long-term revenue, gross margin, profit and cash flow targets for BellSouth's different business units. In general, the business plan prioritised net income and cash flow growth for Bellsouth's different business units. BellSouth's CEO, John Clendenin, reaffirmed BellSouth's continuing commitment to this business plan and its priorities. However, he clarified that BellSouth's core business was telecommunications and that it would only pursue telecommunications opportunities or opportunities aligned to the telecommunications business. He also kept in place the centralised management structure BellSouth had inherited from AT&T, which included centralised control of strategic planning, financial management and Resource Allocation Processes. As a part of this, the corporate development team had shared responsibility with business units for identifying and pursuing business opportunities. The Resource Allocation Process required business units to give 100 per cent of their net income to the corporate office as dividends. The corporate office would then reallocate these resources to business units based on their capacity to achieve financial hurdles or achieve particular strategic objectives. Thus, business units could be allocated more or less operating resources through the normal budgeting process and also be allocated additional strategic resources through the support of the corporate development team for particular strategic initiatives. Through the inherited business plan specifying strategic priorities for Bellsouth and his efforts reaffirming BellSouth's commitment to that business plan and focus on the telecommunications business, BellSouth's CEO clarified the organisation's strategic priorities. In retaining AT&T's successful centralised management structure and Resource Allocation Process, he provided the enabling structures such as measurement and reporting systems, incentive and disincentive systems and administrative mechanisms. From a capabilities and tools perspective, he also inherited and kept AT&T's key capabilities and tools, especially essential ones such as talent, systems, technologies and processes.

Top-down initiatives at BellSouth were the objectives set in the organisation's business plan. These included short, medium and long-term revenue, gross margin, profit and cash flow targets for BellSouth's different business units. BellSouth's corporate office allocated or reallocated resources to these initiatives based on past performance or on anticipated likelihood of these initiatives being realised. The allocation or reallocation of resources occurred through the established budgeting process and/or thorough project proposals that could be submitted through the corporate development team and approved by the top management team. Additional resources to be allocated could either come from existing uncommitted resources reserved for opportunistic commitment to emergent opportunities, from withdrawal of resources previously allocated to initiatives that had limited merit or from business units contributing net income dividends in excess of their business plan targets.

BellSouth's CEO, John Clendenin, made it clear to employees that although BellSouth's core focus was telecommunications, he wanted employees to come up with and pursue opportunities in that core business or complementary to that core business. Having created the strategic context to encourage the emergence of bottom-up initiatives, he also ensured there was the right structural context to encourage their emergence. This structural context included giving the corporate development team shared responsibility with business units for identifying and pursuing business opportunities, ensuring the ongoing availability of uncommitted resources to be able to commit to emerging bottom-up opportunities and ensuring the corporate finance team relaxed stringent profit and cash flow hurdles so nascent initiatives could continue to be allocated resources, if they demonstrated reasonable progress. On top of this, he would personally get involved to support nascent initiatives through actions such as making key hires and giving credibility and authority to those key hires to accelerate their efforts. In undertaking the continuous day-to-day activities of creating and maintaining the strategic and structural context for them, communicating their importance, modelling appropriate leadership behaviours for other senior managers, providing the right resources and incentives and personally getting involved when necessary, John Clendenin ensured an environment was maintained at BellSouth that encouraged the emergence of bottom-up initiatives.

The business plan inherited from AT&T envisioned cellular and other wireless technologies not having much commercial potential. AT&T senior managers had seen wireless as not much more than an "executive toy" and predicted ultimate service penetration of 1 per cent at most. Consequently, most top and middle managers at BellSouth saw cellular technologies as just another of many unregulated opportunities with questionable potential. Bellsouth CEO John Clendenin had supervised an experiment on pre-cellular technology early in his career and had retained an interest in it. When he came across the nascent cellular business unit, he saw it as a complementary business at least, if not a potentially good future business. He decided to give it a helping hand until it could stand on its own. He started by recruiting Bob Tonsfeldt, a key engineering and operations leader at Advanced Mobile Phone Systems (AMPS) to head the mobility business unit. AMPS was a company that was the pioneering leader in mobile phone systems technology. Bob Tonsfeldt, in turn, recruited AMPS' chief strategist, Richard Hohn, who was very enthusiastic about the technology's potential. With the new leadership, the employees of the cellular business unit (known as BellSouth Mobility Incorporated or BMI) began to see the potential of cellular technologies and to get energised by it. John Clendenin further helped the nascent cellular unit along by pushing the corporate finance team to relax the financial hurdles for the AMPS unit to be allocated resources, so as not to over emphasise the need for early profits at the expense of positioning for long-term growth.

The BMI team got to work and invested its efforts in developing a cellular telephone service. When the unit finally introduced this cellular telephone service, it found an unexpectedly strong customer response, with cellular subscribers consistently exceeding expectations. Encouraged by the strong market response, BMI's chief strategist, Richard Hohn, proposed the idea of expanding the cellular telephone business by acquiring out of region cellular licenses. Hohn and Tonsfeldt sought a sponsor from the corporate development team and found Jack Roberts, BellSouth's director of corporate development. When they pitched cellular technology and the acquisitions idea to Jack Roberts, he saw the potential of cellular technology but was still somewhat uncertain. Over time, Hohn resolved his uncertainties and they both developed confidence in each other and started to exchange ideas and plans regarding the cellular business opportunity for BellSouth. As BMI's president, Tonsfeldt supported them by allowing Hohn to work for the corporate development team while still on BMI's payroll.

With Hohn on board, the corporate development team had the strategic and technical expertise to assemble a rigorous business plan for the expansion of the cellular business. This plan was good enough for Roberts to get support from Duane Ackerman, a member of the top management team to which Roberts directly reported. With Ackerman's support, the business plan was successfully pitched to, supported and funded by the executive team. This business plan proposed expansion through a series of acquisitions, with Communication Industries being the first proposed acquisition. Although the executive team had approved this acquisition, Bellsouth ultimately lost out on the deal to Pacific Telesis. But the team quickly moved on to other targets and expansion projects including a 50/50 joint venture with Mobile Communications Corporation of America and an Atlanta-based paging business. With the top management team taking some risk on BMI's initiatives, BMI was careful to make sure it always met corporate's net income and cash flow budgets. Gradually, it started to exceed these budgets and gain more confidence in its initiatives from the top management team.

Cellular phone services eventually started to take off in a big way, and the industry experienced strong unprecedented growth both locally and globally. As they saw their domestic acquisitions boom and competition for potential future acquisitions amplify, Jack Roberts, Richard Hohn and Bob Tonsfeldt started to turn their attention to international wireless opportunities. While it was still too early for cellular in some countries, they were of the firm belief that wireless would eventually be introduced everywhere in the world and they proposed that BellSouth should be a leader in this worldwide market. Unfortunately for the team, at the same time, changes in the corporate senior management team started to occur that saw BMI lose some of its key top management team supporters. In addition, Richard Hohn passed away unexpectedly from cancer in 1987, leaving Jack Roberts and Bob Tonsfeldt to advocate for BellSouth's global cellular strategy. Fortunately for the team that remained, rapidly accelerating growth and superior performance by their existing acquisitions meant they were now consistently over-delivering on BMI's income and cash flow targets. Because of this, it became much easier for the BMI team to get the new corporate team to buy into their global wireless strategy, which was still a big bet to take at the time. BMI was iteratively allocated resources to enter into a joint venture with AirCall Communications in the UK, to acquire Link Communications in Australia, to provide services via TDF Radio Service in France, to compete for and win the franchise for cellular services in Argentina, to compete for the Pan-European cellular licence in Germany and to compete for and win the cellular licence in western Mexico. As BMI continued to deliver positive results from its initiatives, the corporate team grew more and more confident in its leaders and allocated BMI more and more significant resources to continue its expansion. BMI would end up establishing operations across South America, Europe, the Asia-Pacific region and other geographies.

Looking back, BellSouth's CEO did a number of things to shepherd the BMI team from powerful stakeholders and to enable the team to circumvent the regular Resource Allocation Process. First, he had given the BMI team a lot of early public support by taking a personal interest in the team's work, explaining its fit with the existing telecommunications business and ensuring he attracted a capable and well-regarded leader to lead the business. This likely eased potential stifling pressure from powerful stakeholders who may have questioned whether cellular was potentially a wasteful distraction and could have discouraged it. He had ensured that the corporate finance team relaxed what would otherwise have been very restrictive financial hurdles for resource allocation to the nascent team. For instance, if BMI had to meet the standard income and cash flow hurdles that the rest of the business had to meet to continue to get allocated resources, the team may have been more preoccupied with trying to meet those financial hurdles than on focusing on future growth positioning. Finally, the requirement for all businesses to pay 100 per cent of net income as dividends to the corporate office meant that the corporate development team had growing uncommitted resources to allocate outside the regular budgeting process.

John Clendenin's actions demonstrate he was vigilant enough to intervene when the BMI unit was most at risk of being stifled. Although this case study has tracked a single successful bottom-up initiative, in reality a number of initiatives would have been going through this iterated process of resource allocation at BellSouth. These initiatives would have been competing for scarce corporate resources and finite top management attention with varying degrees of success. Those initiatives with early and continued success experienced escalating resource commitments, whereas those with deteriorating success experienced a de-escalation of resource commitments. The role of the top management team in creating the strategic and structural context to encourage the emergence of bottom-up initiatives, of nurturing and shepherding nascent bottom-up initiatives, of ensuring the availability of uncommitted resources (e.g. through reallocation of resources from top-down and bottom-up initiatives) and of being vigilant to and removing obstacles to bottom-up initiatives has been demonstrated.

Are you in the right environment for this process?

The Resource Allocation Process was equally used across obvious, complex, chaotic and high velocity/high volatility environments. However, we found it to be most effective in complex and chaotic environments. While it was still cited to be effective in obvious and complicated environments, cited effectiveness was not as high. Across organisation sizes, the process was used much more in large and small organisations than in medium-sized organisations. Across sectors, the process was used much more within the private sector than in NGO/NFP or government organisations. Therefore, if you are in a large or small organisation within the private sector and your organisation is in a complex, chaotic or high velocity/high volatility environment, this process is likely to be right for you. But there are other issues to consider. Your organisation should have the engagement level necessary to motivate front-line employees to form strategic initiatives and to motivate middle managers to interpret, sponsor and translate those initiatives into a format digestible by senior managers. Also, senior managers need to be able to invest the appropriate time and energy to carry out the strategic leadership activities within this process.

Knowing when you are using it

You are likely to be using the Resource Allocation Process if the eight steps described earlier resemble the steps taken by your organisation to execute strategy. Having a resource allocation approach that runs in parallel to or in place of the traditional budgeting process is also a sign that you may be using the Resource Allocation Process. For example, BellSouth had a process for accumulating uncommitted resources and using these resources for allocation to bottom-up projects submitted via the corporate development team and approved by the top management team. This process ran in parallel to the more traditional budgeting process. Other telltale signs include observations of top managers publicly encouraging employees to form autonomous initiatives, getting personally involved with some very promising initiatives and allocating increasingly larger resources to succeeding initiatives.

Process strengths and shortcomings

We noticed three standout strengths of the Resource Allocation Process. The first was its ability to engage all levels of the organisation in general, and innovators in particular, by providing more autonomy to work on bottom-up initiatives. By pushing part of the strategy making to general managers, operating managers and front-line employees, the process empowers these different stakeholders to think about how they can best contribute to the strategy. In doing so, it fosters greater organisation-wide engagement than if strategy making was limited to the top management team, for example. A second key strength of the Resource Allocation Process is its ability to enable the organisation to adapt to changes in its environment by encouraging the formation, pursuit and realisation of emergent strategic initiatives. Strategy researchers have demonstrated how the formation and realisation of such initiatives by front-line employees, operating managers and general managers can produce the right innovation for the right time to enable the organisation to respond to changes in its external environment. These researchers have also outlined why front-line employees, operating managers and general managers have greater technical, staff, customer and market knowledge than top management and are thus well positioned to see and respond to the need for change earlier. For example, when the top management team at Intel finally realised it was time to get out of the memory business, they were surprised to find that lower level managers had already gotten out of it and come up with alternative products with more promising prospects. All that remained was for the top management team to shut down the flow of research funding into the memory business. A third key strength of the Resource Allocation Process is the potential ease with which it can be run in parallel with other strategy processes to maximise ambidexterity. The process can be run in parallel to, say, the Execution

Premium Process, the 7 Factor Process or any other strategy process. Because of this, it also does not require existing financial management processes to be undone, although strategic leaders may have to encourage relaxation of particular constraints on bottom-up initiatives that these processes may create. The amenability of this process to being operated in parallel with other strategy processes is important since it provides an organisation with an easier opportunity to effect ambidexterity. As we discussed earlier, affecting ambidexterity in turn enables the organisation to make the most of today's business opportunities while at the same time not missing out on tomorrow's opportunities.

There are four potential challenges of using the Resource Allocation Process. The first is that it requires an appropriate level of uncommitted resources to be able to allocate to bottom-up initiatives as these initiatives emerge. Usually, this will require reallocation of resources from top-down or other bottom-up initiatives that have stalling potential. It may also require some other form of ongoing top-up. At BellSouth, all businesses had to pay 100 per cent of their net income as dividends to the corporate office. This meant that the corporate development team had growing uncommitted resources to allocate outside of the regular budgeting process. A second challenge of the Resource Allocation Process is that it may be seen as a disruptive challenge to traditional financial governance and control processes. Perhaps it is because of this that the BellSouth CEO intervened to ensure that existing financial governance and control requirements were relaxed so as not to stifle nascent bottom-up initiatives. Thus, strategic leaders need to think through this challenge, plan for the smooth functioning of both processes and be vigilant to the need for their intervention to resolve potential dysfunction. Third, the Resource Allocation Process' focus on bottom-up initiatives may be a challenge for organisations in environments that prioritise short-term results. You may have observed in the BellSouth case study that while the mobility unit made great contributions to BellSouth's profitability and ultimate survival, it did not do this overnight. In the meantime, the mobility unit was consuming resources. This short-term versus long-term trade-off is essentially the important efficiency and adaptation trade-off we've discussed earlier.

Common tips and traps

To get the best out of this process, we recommend that strategic leaders pay particular attention to determining what the appropriate level of uncommitted resources should be and where these resources will come from. Without availability of such resources, emerging bottom-up initiatives may be stifled and not reach their potential. We also recommend that strategic leaders carefully think through how traditional financial governance and control processes will affect the Resource Allocation Process. That is, will the need for compliance with such processes constrain the development of bottom-up initiatives too much? What should be the appropriate performance expectations of bottom-up initiatives at different stages be to keep them grounded in commercial reality but also not to compromise long-term potential? Finally, we recommend that strategic leaders be vigilant at all times to the need for their intervention in order to nurture, shepherd or start scaling bottom-up initiatives. Our three recommendations would avoid potential traps of encouraging the emergence of bottom-up initiatives, but then losing out on their benefits through lack of resources to invest in them, stifling them through steep financial hurdles/controls or letting them fall prey to the conflicting interests of powerful stakeholders.

Spotlight on the role of strategic leaders

The role of strategic leadership to the proper functioning of this process cannot be overemphasised. While front-line employees, operating managers and general managers form and develop bottom-up initiatives, strategic leaders play a critical role in creating the strategic and structural context to encourage, motivate and enable employees, operating managers and general managers to form and develop these initiatives. You may notice that, in contrast to other strategy execution processes, almost all of the steps and activities of the Resource Allocation Process are for strategic leaders to carry out. The effectiveness of this process largely depends on how routinely and effectively strategic leaders carry out these activities. Tomo Noda and Joseph Bower provide a contrasting example of another of the seven operating companies formed when AT&T was broken up (US West), which also had wireless as a bottom-up initiative but whose strategic leadership ultimately stifled its emergence and thus the ultimate survival of the organisation.

What if you are not a strategic leader?

Even if you are not a strategic leader, this process puts you front and centre of strategy formation and realisation. If you come up with an important initiative to your organisation's future, there are almost no limits to how far such an initiative can catapult you within your organisation or within your industry. But where do you start? We suggest you start to constantly consider questions such as: what problems are my organization's current and potential customers having? What new products/services or existing product/service improvements could solve these problems? What new product/service innovations could be introduced in my organisation's current and potential markets? What process or technology changes could be initiated in my organisation that could improve its efficiency and effectiveness? What internal and external changes are occurring and what opportunities or threats are these creating for my organisation? What technological breakthroughs should my organisation apply to improve its current product or service offerings? What new business opportunities do recent innovations within my team or within another part of the organisation create?

You can discuss any insights that occur from considering such questions with other people within the organisation to find potential collaborators to help further develop your ideas. Once you have developed your ideas to a certain point, you might want to consider pitching them to your line manager or to an operating manager or general manager at your organisation so as to seek sponsors who can help you further develop your ideas into prototype solutions and or suggest ways to align those solutions with the organisation's strategy. While most of your ideas may not get much traction, over time you will conceive better ideas, and one or more of these could turn out to be the critical bottom-up initiative that changes your organisation's destiny.

Notes

1 Bower, J. L. (1970). *Managing the resource allocation process.* Boston, MA: Harvard Business School Press.
2 Bower, J., & Gilbert, C. (2007). How managers' everyday decisions create—or destroy—your company's strategy. *Harvard Business Review,* February.
3 Bower, J. L. (1970). *Managing the resource allocation process.* Boston, MA: Harvard Business School Press.
4 Burgelman, R. A. (1983). A model of the interaction of strategic behavior, corporate context, and the concept of strategy. *Academy of Management Review, 8*(1), 61–70.
5 Sull, D. N. (1999). The dynamics of standing still: Firestone Tire & Rubber and the radial revolution. *Business History Review, 73*(3), 430–464.
6 Christensen, C. M., & Bower, J. L. (1996). Customer power, strategic investment, and the failure of leading firms. *Strategic Management Journal, 17,* 197–218.
7 Bower, J. L. (1970). *Managing the resource allocation process.* Boston, MA: Harvard Business School Press.
8 Bower, J. L., & Gilbert, C. G. (Eds.). (2005). *From resource allocation to strategy.* Oxford: Oxford University Press.

9 Bower, J., & Gilbert, C. (2007). How managers' everyday decisions create—or destroy—your company's strategy. *Harvard Business Review*, February.
10 Burgelman, R. A. (1983). A model of the interaction of strategic behavior, corporate context, and the concept of strategy. *Academy of Management Review*, *8*(1), 61–70.
11 Bower, J. L., & Gilbert, C. G. (Eds.). (2005). *From resource allocation to strategy*. Oxford: Oxford University Press.
12 Noda, T., & Bower, J. L. (1996). Strategy making as iterated processes of resource allocation. *Strategic Management Journal, 17*(S1), 159–192.
13 Mui, C. (2012). The lesson that market leaders are failing to learn from Xerox PARC. *Forbes*, February.
14 Noda, T., & Bower, J. L. (1996). Strategy making as iterated processes of resource allocation. *Strategic Management Journal, 17*(S1), 159–192.

8 The Simple Rules Process

Origin and design principles

Origin

The Simple Rules Process was developed by Kathleen Eisenhardt and Donald Sull in the course of their research on why certain technology firms thrived while others did not. Kathleen Eisenhardt is a long-standing professor of strategy and management at Stanford University's school of engineering, as well as co-director of the Stanford Technology Ventures Program. Donald Sull is a strategy and management professor at London Business School and formerly at Harvard Business School. His early career was in management consulting with McKinsey and Company and later in private equity investment. These two researchers first identified[1] that technology firms operated in high-velocity environments, and that such environments were characterised by extraordinary complexity, high-velocity change and fleeting opportunity windows. They subsequently discovered that successful firms in such environments were those able to make on-the-spot decisions, adapt to rapidly changing circumstances and, at the same time, keep these decisions and actions aligned to a big picture strategy. They translated this requirement for effectiveness in such environments into what they called the establishment and use of "Simple Rules". We have in turn translated their findings into the Simple Rules Process. This process involves determining, communicating and enabling the use of simple rules of thumb to seize fleeting opportunities and realise strategy rather than relying on complicated frameworks.

The problem

Although Eisenhardt and Sull initially sought to understand why certain technology companies thrived while others did not, they soon turned their attention to the challenges of high-velocity environments and how firms can navigate and thrive in such environments. They discovered that sustained effectiveness in such environments required enabling leaders to make on-the-spot decisions and to adapt to rapidly changing circumstances while, at the same time, keeping these decisions and actions aligned to a big picture strategy. Eisenhardt and Sull propose that the Simple Rules Process provides a solution to another important but unaddressed strategy issue. They argue that for strategy to influence action it has to be remembered; for it to be remembered it has to first be understood; and for it to be understood, it has to be simple.[2] Thus, the Simple Rules Process provides a solution to the common challenge of strategies being too complicated to be understood. It does this by providing a way for strategic leaders to distil a potentially complicated strategy into a simple set of rules that can be understood, remembered and acted on by people in all parts of the organisation as they make on-the-spot decisions and adapt to changing circumstances.

The idea in brief

The key steps in the Simple Rules Process are as follows: (1) set clear direction by clarifying the priority strategic objectives, (2) identify bottlenecks that may keep the organisation from achieving strategic objectives, and (3) effect simple rules for dealing with the bottlenecks. Here, we unpack and justify each of these Simple Rules Process steps based on Kathleen Eisenhardt and Donald Sull's research over more than two decades (see Figure 8.1).

   Step 1: Set clear direction by clarifying the priority strategic objectives – The aim of the Simple Rules Process is to enable employees to make on-the-spot decisions, improvise and adapt to rapidly changing circumstances while keeping these decisions and actions aligned to a big picture strategy. For them to keep their decisions and actions aligned to this big picture strategy, they need to understand it and then remember it. Thus, Step 1 of the Simple Rules Process focuses on clarifying this big picture strategy and translating it into a format that can be easily understood and remembered by employees. Achieving this first requires that strategic leaders get an intimate understanding of their internal and external environment and thus the immediate, medium and long-term opportunities and threats faced by their organisation. Having done this, they can then identify the critical three or four strategic objectives that can drive a wedge between revenues and costs and therefore come up with a plan to maximise profitability and longevity. They then need to ensure that these three or four priority strategic objectives are translated into a format that will be most understandable, compelling and memorable for their employees.

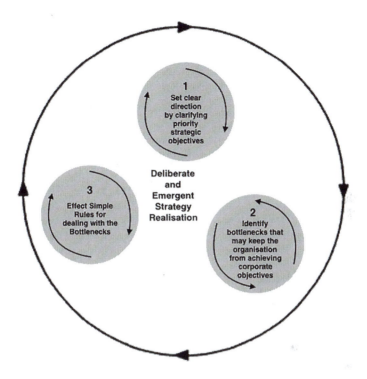

Figure 8.1 The Simple Rules Process.

Step 2: Identify the bottlenecks that may keep the organisation from achieving its priority strategic objectives – Eisenhardt and Sull use the term bottleneck to describe activities, decisions or situations that are likely to hinder an organisation's employees from achieving the organisation's priority strategic objectives. The term "bottleneck" is used in the engineering field to describe a system component that limits the performance of the system. For example, the slowest activity in a production line may set the maximum efficiency possible for the production line. In the Simple Rules approach, a bottleneck can be any limited resource, like doctors' time in a volunteer medical service. Thus, Step 2 of the Simple Rules Process is concerned with identifying the critical bottlenecks to achieve the priority strategic objectives. Eisenhardt and Sull propose that strategic leaders focus on identifying and honing in on the critical bottlenecks among a potential multitude that may derail achievement of the priority strategic objectives. Bottlenecks need to be defined narrowly and not be ambiguous. For this to happen, they usually need to be defined as specific processes, process steps or activities that can be stopped, started, modified or circumvented. They can also be defined as specific resources that need to be allocated, outcomes that need to be achieved first (e.g. winning over more of a particular type of client), events that need to occur (e.g. quality reviews), events that need to stop occurring or strategic factors[3] (i.e. critical things the organisation must excel at).

Step 3: Effect simple rules for dealing with the bottlenecks – Having identified the critical bottlenecks that are likely to derail achievement of the organisation's priority strategic objectives, Step 3 focuses on how to prevent them getting in the way of achieving those priority strategic objectives. This is done by forming and effecting simple rules to guide the organisation's employees on how to deal with the bottlenecks as they arise (or upgrading the Simple Rules that already exist). Eisenhardt and Sull recommend that, rather than devising and effecting top-down rules, strategic leaders should assemble an appropriately diverse team to craft the Simple Rules. They add that such a team ought to include the people who will be using the rules on a day-to-day basis. Such people are likely to have a more intimate understanding of the situation on the ground, to strike the right balance between guidance and discretion and to phrase rules in the appropriate language for the audience that will be using them. Examples of Simple Rules used in different organisations are abundant. For example, the Oakland A's (the US professional baseball team based in Oakland, California) had simple rules for their talent scouts such as "No high school players" and "No players with problems that the club cannot fix". IDEO, the international design and consulting firm, has simple rules such as "Encourage wild ideas" and "Go for quantity" to guide its idea generation processes. Pracuj, a leading Brazilian recruitment firm, had "Any new product must support at least one of the company's current priorities" and that a new project would only be considered if it "introduces a new feature that supports the company's vision, has been proven in another market, and could be tested on a limited scale". You may be able to easily imagine the types of bottlenecks that resulted in these rules being formed and effected.

Caveats

As with other processes, the Simple Rules Process steps are not episodic and sequential but always at work, even if some steps may have to start before others. The activities within the three steps and the ongoing updating of the outcomes of those activities are the daily responsibility of strategic leaders. The iterative nature of the process enables the real-time updating of the organisation's priority strategic objectives, of identifying the critical obstacles needing new rules or existing rules needing modification, of effecting new rules required and of retirement of obsolete rules.

What you might know it as

If you are familiar with the literature on the use of heuristics in organisations, for example, using heuristics for adaptive decision-making, aspects of the Simple Rules may already be familiar to you. Similarly, aspects of the Simple Rules Process may seem similar to academic and practitioner literature on principles-based management, business rules management and policy-based management. While the prescriptions in these literatures may resonate with the prescriptions of the Simple Rules Process, the Simple Rules Process differs in that it is specifically focused on strategy execution enablement. The process and its rules are aimed at effecting the optimal amount of constraint on action to optimise the realisation of both deliberate and emergent strategy.

Prevalence

We found 18 per cent of organisations, or about one in every five organisations, using the Simple Rules Process to execute strategy. The process was used more in the private and NGO/NFP sectors than the public/government sector. Across organisation sizes, the smaller the organisation, the more likely it was to use the Simple Rules Process. Perhaps this is because in large organisations there are so many different services/products, markets, and processes that using the Simple Rules Process in isolation may prove a challenge. Where large organisations used the Simple Rules Process, we often found it used in parallel with other processes. The process was mostly associated with high execution effectiveness in complicated and complex environments. Our research suggests that it can be a very effective process. Across all environments, about half of organisations making extensive use of the process cited "above peers" execution effectiveness and the other half cited "same as peers" execution effectiveness (see Figure 8.2).

The process in action

To demonstrate the Simple Rules Process in action, we use the case study of a large railway and logistics company in Brazil that used the process for an urgent turnaround agenda. As you read the case, pay attention to the outcomes of the organisation's approach to the Simple

Process	Sector				Employees (Org Size)				
	Public Sector / Government	Private Sector	NGO/NFP	All Sectors	>500	51-499	2 - 50	<2	All Sizes
7 Factor Process	10%	13%	25%	13%	19%	10%	10%	0%	12%
Execution Premium Process	24%	16%	25%	18%	25%	21%	13%	11%	18%
Simple Rules	14%	20%	17%	18%	13%	21%	23%	44%	21%
Lean Strategy Deployment Process	14%	19%	25%	18%	22%	21%	15%	11%	18%
Change Acceleration Process	14%	11%	17%	12%	9%	21%	10%	11%	12%
Project Management Process	53%	80%	66%	70%	88%	84%	63%	33%	72%
Talent Placement Process	14%	27%	25%	23%	22%	26%	23%	11%	22%
Outcomes and Incentives / Disincentives Communication Process	24%	28%	25%	26%	31%	26%	25%	11%	26%
Learning on the Run Process	39%	38%	50%	38%	31%	42%	43%	22%	37%
Resource Allocation / Portfolio Management Process	19%	17%	25%	18%	22%	21%	18%	66%	24%
Performance Monitoring and Feedback Process	39%	38%	50%	38%	44%	37%	43%	0%	38%

Figure 8.2 Proportion of study participants citing use of the Simple Rules Process by sector and organisation size.*

Note: *For example, of the 241 study participants, 50 participants were from the public sector/government. Of these 50 public sector/government participants, 5 participants (10%) used the 7 Factor Process. This table differs from Tables 6.23 and 6.24 shown in Busulwa (2016), where process users in each sector are shown as a proportion of all study participants. So, in the case of public sector/government users of the 7 Factor Process, this is shown as 2% (i.e. 5/241 = 2%).

Rules Process. Also consider the organisation's unique setting and the potential challenges of this setting for the Simple Rules Process. As you review the case, if you believe the Simple Rules Process suits your organisation's setting, you may be able to adapt some of the approaches in the case study to form your organisation's unique approach to the process. If the process does not suit your organisation, there may be particular strategy execution insights and practices that you can pick up and adapt to whatever approach you choose to take to strategy execution.

Case study: using simple rules at Rumo: the urgent turnaround of a railway and logistics giant[4]

Rumo is a Brazilian logistics and transportation organisation and the largest railway logistics company in Latin America. In the 1990s, Brazil's freight rail infrastructure was run down. Half of the bridges were in need of repair and almost one-fifth were near collapse. In 1997, the Brazilian government privatised its freight lines by spinning off Rumo, or América Latina Logística, as it was called then, from the Brazilian Railway Authority. The new management team inherited an overstaffed bureaucratic organisation that was bleeding cash.

The CEO adopted a Simple Rules approach to the work before the executive team and began the first step of setting strategic objectives. The executive team discussed the issues before them and decided on four strategic objectives as priorities: cut costs, grow revenue by expanding services to existing customers, invest selectively to improve infrastructure and build an aggressive corporate culture. The executive team identified capital budgeting as the critical bottleneck, particularly for upgrading infrastructure and expanding services. With these insights, the CEO put together a cross-functional team to come up with simple rules for prioritising capital expenditure.

The cross-functional team determined that every capital expenditure proposal needed to conform to four simple rules. It had to:

1   Remove obstacles to revenue growth
2   Minimise upfront expenditure
3   Provide immediate rather than long-term payoff
4   Reuse existing resources

These simple rules translated the strategic objectives into clear guidelines that managers and their people could understand and act on. A number of innovative but rule compliant proposals arose from the ground up. For example, one employee proposed increasing the size of fuel tanks to expand the distance engines could go without refuelling, thus reducing downtime during peak harvest season, a period when large amounts of harvest had previously been left to rot due to downtime. Past proposals had been imposed in a top-down manner, resulting in silos, hidden agendas and distrust. Since the rules were put together by a cross-functional team, they functioned like agreements across different parts of the organisation. And what may have otherwise been a disengaging and anxiety-provoking period became one of energy and vitality. While the simple rules didn't eliminate every trade-off, they provided a framework for productive discussion and resolution. Within 3 years, Rumo's revenue increased by 50 per cent and its earnings before interest, tax, depreciation, and amortisation (EBITDA) tripled. Within another 4 years, Rumo had become one of the best employers in Brazil and was admired for its performance culture.

Are you in the right environment for this process?

The Simple Rules Process was distilled from the practices of effective organisations in high-velocity environments. These were environments characterised by extraordinary complexity, rapid change and fleeting windows of opportunity. Therefore, if you are in such an environment, you are most likely in the right environment for this process. However, we found it to be most effective in complicated and complex environments. While it was still cited to be effective in obvious and chaotic environments, our research suggests that its effectiveness was not as high. The process was largely used to the same degree across all organisation sizes, except in small business organisations, where the usage rate was double that of other organisation sizes. Across sectors, the process was used more in the private sector. Thus, if you are in a small business within the private sector and your organisation is in a complicated, complex or chaotic environment, then this process is likely to be well suited to you.

Knowing when you are using it

You are likely to be using the Simple Rules Process if the three steps described earlier resemble the steps taken by your organisation to execute strategy. If you are using heuristics-based management, principles-based management, business rules management, policy-based management and some forms of contemporary management control systems, you may find using Simple Rules a natural extension of what you already know. Use of the Simple Rules Process is synonymous with regular and ongoing discussion of bottlenecks and of rules to resolve bottlenecks. It is also synonymous with employees pursuing both deliberate and emergent strategic actions to enable seizure of both today's and tomorrow's fleeting opportunities. Thus, if you apply implicit or explicit rules to undertake autonomous improvisatory actions, it is likely you are using simple rules to some degree – even if not explicitly.

Process strengths and shortcomings

We found four standout strengths of the Simple Rules Process. The first is the process' ability to push opportunity recognition, on-the-spot decision-making and improvisatory action to all parts of the business to enable local responsiveness. In doing so, the process empowers these parts of the organisation to adapt to rapidly changing local circumstances and to seize fleeting opportunities in near to real time. Second, the Simple Rules Process enables strategic leaders to tailor the amount of structure, or level of constraint on the improvisatory actions of employees, through the number and the nature of the simple rules in place. In doing so, it better enables strategic leaders to shape the amount of structure to what best optimises the mix of deliberate and emergent strategies being realised. For example, strategic leaders who want to increase the realisation of deliberate strategies may go for more simple rules and rules that constrain action more. In contrast, strategic leaders who want to increase the realisation of emergent strategies may want fewer rules or rules with less constraints on the actions of employees. In enabling strategic leaders to shape the realisation of both deliberate and emergent strategy, the Simple Rules Process puts the ambidexterity leaver in their hands. The third standout strength of the Simple Rules Process is its ability to provide a way for strategic leaders to distil potentially complicated strategies into a set of objectives and rules that can be understood, remembered and acted on by people in all parts of the organisation. Having employees understand, remember and act on an organisation's strategy has been a long-standing challenge to successful strategy execution. Finally, the Simple Rules Process has the ability to foster improvisation or autonomous actions that are aligned to the organisation's desired strategic direction. This is also an important strength since strategic alignment has been another long-standing challenge to successful strategy execution.

We found some shortcomings of the Simple Rules Process. First, many potential process users raised concern that loosening of managerial control to drive realisation of deliberate strategy may result in diminished ability to realise such strategy. Or, alternatively, it may require much better engagement and leadership at lower levels of the organisation or parts of the organisation very removed from the reach of the executive team. Second, prospective process users in large complex organisations raised concern that in large complex organisations subject to intense performance pressures, reliability that deliberate strategy will be released may be greatly diminished. Other prospective process users raised concerns about the greater political/legal risk that may come with the process' use in highly regulated and politicized environments.

Common tips and traps

Eisenhardt and Sull encapsulate the common tips and traps into some simple rules to stick to when identifying bottlenecks, forming and effecting simple rules. The first rule is to "identify bottlenecks that are both specific and strategic". That is, bottlenecks should be relatively narrow and well-defined processes, process steps, activities, events or non-events. This helps make the resultant rules specific and explicit rather than being vague; for example, the rule "A project can only be considered if it introduces a new feature that supports the company's vision, has been proven in another market, and can be tested on a limited scale" is better than "Recognise and reward quality improvement practices". In the latter rule, you may be able to tell that the bottlenecks identified were not specific enough or strategic enough. The second rule they propose is that "Data should trump opinion". That is, when identifying bottlenecks or forming rules or evaluating the effectiveness of rules, data should be used over opinions. Third, they propose that "Users make the rules". That is, people who will use the rules are better placed to craft them as they can strike the appropriate balance between understandability, guidance, limitation and cumbersomeness. This is as opposed to senior management just dictating the rules. Having users craft the rules does not stop management from selecting the appropriate team of users or from undertaking review and approval of the rules. The fourth rule is that "Rules should be concrete". That is, the rules should result in a clear yes or no, rather than being ambiguous or subjective. Finally, Eisenhardt and Sull propose that "The rules should evolve". They provide examples of teams that meet regularly to review the rules for ongoing relevance, effectiveness and need for modification or replacement.

Spotlight on the role of strategic leaders

As we have previously discussed, a fundamental role of strategic leaders is to ensure the realisation of strategies that balance the efficient pursuit or mitigation of today's opportunities and threats with building capacity to adapt to tomorrow's threats and opportunities. Discharging this fundamental role in the Simple Rules Process requires strategic leaders to ensure that the most important strategic objectives are identified, prioritised and translated into a format that every employee can understand, remember and act on. Having achieved this, strategic leaders then need to be vigilant to the bottleneck identification and rules formation to ensure that the rules formed and effected result in the optimal realisation of deliberate and emergent strategies to maximise the organisation's longevity. Both these responsibilities are the ongoing, day in and day out tasks of strategic leaders using this process. The efficiency and effectiveness with which strategic leaders carry out these tasks determines the efficiency and effectiveness with which the organisation realises deliberate and emergent strategies. The efficiency and effectiveness with which an organisation realises deliberate and emergent strategies ultimately determines its fate.

What if you are not a strategic leader?

If you are not a strategic leader, this is another process that puts you front and centre of strategy formation and realisation. Once you have a good understanding of your organisation's priority strategic objectives and simple rules, this process enables you to think up ideas and to collaborate with others on shaping those ideas into strategic initiatives that support the organisation's priority strategic objectives and comply with the Simple Rules. Similar to the Resource Allocation process, if you come up with an important initiative to your organisation's future, there are almost no limits to how far such an initiative can catapult you within your organisation or within your industry. We suggest you start to constantly consider questions such as: what problems are my organization's current and potential customers having? What new products/services or existing product/service improvements could solve these problems? What new product/service innovations could be introduced in my organisation's current and potential markets? What process or technology changes could be initiated in my organisation that could improve its efficiency and effectiveness? What internal and external changes are occurring and what opportunities or threats are these creating for my organisation? What technological breakthroughs should my organisation apply to improve its current product or service offerings? What new business opportunities do recent innovations within my team or within another part of the organisation create? You can discuss any insights that occur from considering such questions with other people within the organisation to find potential collaborators to help further develop your ideas. Once you have developed your ideas to a certain point, you might want to consider pitching them to your line manager or to an operating manager or general manager at your organisation so as to seek sponsors that can help you further develop your ideas into prototype solutions and suggest ways to align those solutions with the organisation's strategy. While most of your ideas may not get much traction, over time you will conceive better and better ideas, and one or more or your ideas could turn out to be the critical Simple Rules initiative that changes your organisation's fate.

Notes

1 Sull, D., & Eisenhardt, K. (2012, September). Simple Rules for a complex world. *Harvard Business Review, 90*(9), 68.
2 Sull, D., & Eisenhardt, K. (2012, September). Simple Rules for a complex world. *Harvard Business Review, 90*(9), 68.
3 Kenny, G. (2014). A list of goals is not a strategy. *Harvard Business Review.* Retrieved from https://hbr.org/2014/11/a-list-of-goals-is-not-a-strategy
4 Sull, D., & Eisenhardt, K. (2012, September). Simple Rules for a complex world. *Harvard Business Review, 90*(9), 68.

9 The Learning on the Run or Strategic Learning Process

Origin and design principles

Origin

As discussed in Chapter 1, we used case study interviews to ask executive, middle management and front-line employees across different parts of the value chain to describe the steps involved in executing strategy at their organization. While many study participants described processes consistent with academic research or the practitioner literature, four of the processes discovered were not apparent in either academic research or the practitioner literature. The Learning on the Run Process was one of these four processes. Users described the process as one of choosing a general direction and implementing in that direction by rapidly pursuing opportunities, navigating obstacles, learning from these experiences and continuously adjusting course. On revisiting the research and practitioner literature, we found abundant indirect practitioner literature referencing this process' steps. For example, former General Electric CEO and Jack Welch Management Institute chairman Jack Welch proposed, "In real life, strategy is actually very straightforward. You pick a general direction and you implement like hell".[1] And former Asda and Pandora CEO Allan Leighton proposed that "Strategy is important but it's a compass not a roadmap".[2] In the academic literature, the process echoes the findings of researchers such as Ashridge Strategy Professor James Moncrieff, who described strategy realisation as the interaction of the processes of strategic intent, response to emergent environmental issues, the dynamics of the actions of individuals within the organisation, responses to emergent environmental issues and alignment of action with strategic intent and strategic learning.[3] Other researchers, such as Oxford Professor Eric Beinhocker, have stressed the importance of continuous motion over reliance on a strategy that may be based on inaccurate predictions of the future.[4]

The problem

The Learning on the Run Process addresses the issue of what strategic leaders can do if they face significant uncertainty about what the strategy should be. This could be due to many factors. For example, it could be because strategic leaders are operating in a setting with enough complicatedness, complexity, velocity or volatility that it is difficult to make accurate predictions about what the immediate, medium or long-term future will be. Alternatively, it may be that the strategic leadership team is new to a particular business or environment. In any case, strategic leaders will have questions such as: should any strategic actions be taken? Or should they do nothing and wait for more certainty? If they choose to act instead, what strategic actions should be taken? In such situations, the Learning on the Run Process prescribes choosing a general strategic direction based on the best information strategic leaders are able to access at a point in time and identifying and pursuing potential strategic opportunities aligned to that direction. The strategic direction can be modified, and strategic opportunities can be abandoned or their resource commitment escalated or de-escalated as more certainty emerges.

The idea in brief

The key steps in the Learning on the Run Process are: (1) choose a strategic direction, (2) identify strategic opportunities aligned to that direction, (3) pursue opportunities as insights emerge on what actions to take and how to navigate obstacles, and (4) learn from outcomes and update the strategic direction and opportunities being pursued. What follows is the unpacking and justification of each step based on the findings from our field interviews and questionnaire surveys with executive, middle management and front-line employees (Figure 9.1).

Step 1: Choose a strategic direction – In this step, strategic leaders undertake the continuous monitoring and evaluation of the external and internal environment necessary to identify immediate, medium- and long-term threats and opportunities. Having identified current and future opportunities and threats, they can then speculate on possible future states of their internal and external environments in general and their industry or specific products and services in particular. Armed with this information, strategic leaders can choose a general strategic

Figure 9.1 The Learning on the Run or Strategic Learning Process.

direction to pursue. Such general strategic direction may be in the form of a vision or a mission for the organisation. Alternatively, it could be in the form of an overall objective, strategic objective or set of rules, or even a single rule.

Step 2: Identify strategic opportunities aligned to that direction – This step requires the identification or formation of short and medium-term deliverables that will best contribute to progress towards organisation's strategic direction. Such deliverables can be target outcomes, projects or activities. For instance, this could be a deliverable such as "Successfully raise at least $50 million in funding from a top-tier venture capital firm to effectively scale the business before the patent lapses". Or it could be a project such as "Delivery of the smart lock joint venture project on time, to quality and within budget". Alternatively, it could be an activity such as "Attract an industry esteemed CTO to lead the digital transformation effort".

Step 3: Pursue opportunities as insights emerge on what actions to take and how to navigate obstacles – In this step, action is taken to realise the strategic opportunities identified in step 2. When there is enough uncertainty, such actions may not always be apparent. For instance, the identified strategic opportunity to "Raise $50 million in funding from a top-tier venture capital firm" may be an extremely difficult feat, depending on the nature of the business at the time it identifies this strategic opportunity and the location of the business location. As a result, it may not be clear what actions will lead to realising this opportunity or what the sequencing of those actions should be. But with time, action and strategic learning, insights start to emerge to strategic leaders regarding what actions to take and how to overcome obstacles sure to emerge as those actions are taken. Thus, strategic leaders simply identify some initial actions that can be taken towards the realisation of strategic opportunities, effect these actions, continuously learn from what is working and not working and continuously update the actions being taken as new insights emerge.

Step 4: Learn from outcomes and update the strategic direction and opportunities being pursued – The more and better the actions taken in Step 3, the faster strategic leaders will realise outcomes from these actions. The outcomes of these actions may, in turn, result in the realisation of strategic opportunities and the strategic direction. Often, the outcomes of these actions result in strategic leaders realising that the previously identified strategic direction and/or strategic opportunities were off the mark. In either case, this is a time for strategic leaders to learn from the intended and unintended outcomes of their actions and to upgrade the strategic direction, the opportunities being pursued and the actions being taken in light of that learning.

Caveats

Like other strategy execution processes, the Learning on the Run Process steps are not episodic and sequential. That is, there is no implication that strategy execution is neat, linear and sequential or that strategy formation and implementation are different and separate phases of strategy realisation. Rather, the key steps and activities identified should be taken as iterative processes that happen in organisations every day. For example, Step 4, "Learn from outcomes and update the strategic direction and opportunities being pursued", is the daily task of leaders who wish to ensure that they have the right strategic direction and are recognising, pursuing and realising the opportunities that best accelerate action towards that direction. Also, there is no suggestion that this process should be used in isolation or that it can't be complemented by other activities. For instance, it may be beneficial to operate other strategy processes in parallel or to complement it with generic strategy execution activities such as "strategy communication" or "resource allocation/reallocation".

What you might know it as

You may find aspects of the Learning on the Run Process similar to some of the academic and practitioner literature on strategic learning.[5,6]

This process also shares common elements with quality management and Hoshin Planning, each emphasizing closed-loop and double-loop learning processes. You might notice that the Hoshin Planning and Simple Rules Processes, identified earlier, each emphasise key aspects of the Learning on the Run Process. Generally, we found that many of the strategy execution processes have common elements albeit different focal points.

Prevalence

Across all sectors, we found 38 per cent of organisations, or one in every three organisations, using the Learning on the Run Process. While used across all sectors, the process was most commonly cited by the NGO/NFP sector (50% of such organisations), but public sector/government and private sector use was not far behind (38%). We found that the smaller the organisation, the more likely it was that the Learning on the Run Process was in use. The process had mixed results with regard to strategy execution effectiveness. It was mostly associated with high to very high execution effectiveness in obvious and complicated environments. Its effectiveness in complex and chaotic environments was ambiguous; that is, half the time it was associated with high execution effectiveness and half the time with unclear to low execution effectiveness (see Figure 9.2).

	Sector				Employees (Org Size)				
Process	Public Sector / Government	Private Sector	NGO/NFP	All Sectors	>500	51-499	2 - 50	<2	All Sizes
7 Factor Process	10%	13%	25%	13%	19%	10%	10%	0%	12%
Execution Premium Process	24%	16%	25%	18%	25%	21%	13%	11%	18%
Simple Rules	14%	20%	17%	18%	13%	21%	23%	44%	21%
Lean Strategy Deployment Process	14%	19%	25%	18%	22%	21%	15%	11%	18%
Change Acceleration Process	14%	11%	17%	12%	9%	21%	10%	11%	12%
Project Management Process	53%	80%	66%	70%	88%	84%	63%	33%	72%
Talent Placement Process	14%	27%	25%	23%	22%	26%	23%	11%	22%
Outcomes and Incentives / Disincentives Communication Process	24%	28%	25%	26%	31%	26%	25%	11%	26%
Learning on the Run Process	39%	38%	50%	38%	31%	42%	43%	22%	37%
Resource Allocation / Portfolio Management Process	19%	17%	25%	18%	22%	21%	18%	66%	24%
Performance Monitoring and Feedback Process	39%	38%	50%	38%	44%	37%	43%	0%	38%

Figure 9.2 Proportion of study participants citing use of the Learning on the Run or Strategic Learning Process by sector and organisation size.*

Note: *For example, of the 241 study participants, 50 participants were from the public sector/government. Of these 50 public sector/government participants, 5 participants (10%) used the 7 Factor Process. This table differs from Tables 6.23 and 6.24 shown in Busulwa (2016), where process users in each sector are shown as a proportion of all study participants. So, in the case of public sector/government users of the 7 Factor Process, this is shown as 2% (i.e. 5/241 = 2%).

The process in action

To demonstrate the Learning on the Run Process in action, we have used the case of an early-stage Internet of Things (IoT) company introducing smart lock products. Given the newness of the company's product at the time, its industry is opaque. It is partly in the high-velocity IT industry which is characterised by extraordinary complexity, rapid or high-velocity change and fleeting opportunity windows. But it is also partly in the electronic security and accommodation industries. As you read the case, pay attention to how the company approaches each step of the process and the particular challenges it faces in doing so. Also consider the organisation's unique context, the challenges of this context for the Learning on the Run Process and how the company overcomes these challenges. Even if the process does not suit your particular context, you may find particular strategy execution insights and practices that you can pick up from the case study and adapt to whatever process your organisation uses.

Case study: using the Learning on the Run Process in an early stage firm – pursuing the IoT smart locks opportunity

Joel is the founder of a smart lock start-up based in Australia. When Joel first came up with the product concept, it was just him and he was unclear on how to further develop the concept. For example, he was not very clear on which industry the product fit into. In addition to this, he had no money to finance product development or other basic start-up costs. But he knew his idea had promise, as he had travelled through hotels around the world and been struck by the challenges of physical keys and of electronic key cards. He spoke with as many people as he could about his idea and participated in some government-run business creation and entrepreneurship workshops. Most of the advice he received pointed to the need for assembling a team and entering business planning competitions to help further refine the idea; and win some funding to develop the idea to a point where it might be investable.

Having travelled through different hotels around the world, Joel had a vision of his digital locks being used by hotels to overcome check-in difficulties from lost keys, late arrivals and busy periods. While implicit in his mind, this was Joel's initial strategic direction: that is, the creation of a digital lock to enable hotels to simplify, automate and speed up their check-in process and the subsequent guest access to rooms – a direction very similar to the online check-in service for the airline industry. Having a strategic direction, Joel set about the process of identifying the best strategic opportunities to pursue that were aligned to this strategic direction. Having received much advice to enter business planning competitions, he identified this as his priority strategic opportunity and immediately started to look for local and international business planning competitions that he could enter. As he entered these business planning competitions, Joel noticed that most of them asked questions about his team and some even mandated a team for the application to be considered. Learning from the process of entering business planning competitions and the outcomes of some of the business planning competitions, Joel identified a second strategic opportunity: building a start-up team. He made this his first priority and set about finding appropriate people to join the team. Not having done this before, he stumbled through it using trial and error and opportunism. He was lucky to have one of the business planning competition organisers suggest a potential team member. He made this the first task of the team-building opportunity, and he quickly organised to meet with the potential team member to evaluate his fit and, if suitable, to pitch him on joining the team. Joel succeeded in pitching Luke to become a team member. As Joel was discussing the team-building project with Luke, Luke advised Joel that he had a contact, James, with appropriate skills, who might be interested in joining the team.

Learning from the outcome of the first task, Joel made this the second task and pursued it quickly by meeting with James, evaluating his suitability and pitching him on joining the team. James joined the team and, together, he, Luke and Joel formed the initial founding team. Joel discussed the strategic direction with James and Luke and, as a team, they focused on identifying promising business planning competitions they could enter, entering those competitions, learning from the outcomes and escalating their efforts to achieve even better outcomes. With each subsequent business planning competition, the team learned more about their product, their potential customers and the business opportunity in front of them. They also gradually started to win business planning competitions and acquire funds to further develop the team's product. Each competition the team participated in brought new contacts with ideas on what the team could do to further develop the business. Joel acted quickly to motivate the team to act on each of these ideas, and the team had some great opportunities emerge as a result of these ideas. But some of the ideas they acted on become dead ends.

After many business planning competitions, the team refined its strategic direction and reconfigured its strategic initiatives portfolio. The strategic direction was refined to "become venture capital investment ready as fast as possible". Joel and the team identified three priority strategic opportunities: getting worldwide patents for the smart lock concept, pursuing licencing-based revenue and finding a top manufacturing partner to manufacture prototypes. Joel and his team were energised by the new strategic direction and the mandate to seek out and act on any actions that might deliver on the three priority strategic opportunities they had identified. Over a 5-year period, the team was able to achieve the three priorities through a range of unexpected opportunities that emerged and were pursued. Many of these emerged from the most unexpected places while on the course of pursuing other related objectives. Of course, many obstacles also emerged, but these were overcome through continuous adjustments, improvisation, experimentation and learning. The team was eventually offered a buyout by a stock exchange-listed IoT company. At the time of our study, the team was still considering whether to accept this buyout proposal. Looking back, Joel observed that he couldn't have conceived early on how his idea could go from concept to where the business had gotten to; only through setting a working direction, rapidly identifying and pursuing potential strategic opportunities, learning from successes and failures and adjusting course in real time could he have succeeded as a strategic leader.

Are you in the right environment for this process?

Although most commonly used by the NGO/NFP sector, we found the Learning on the Run Process to have high usage across all sectors and organisation sizes and to be associated with high execution effectiveness in a range of environments. It was particularly effective in obvious and complicated environments but had either very high or very low execution effectiveness in complex and chaotic environments. Thus, if you are in obvious or complicated environments, this process is likely to suit your setting; if you are in a complex or chaotic setting, then it may have applicability to your situation, but it is worth using with vigilance. Study participants suggested this process was effective in large complex organisations but, if not used in conjunction with other strategy processes, we are concerned about its ability to overcome the complex governance, administrative and communication structures of such organisations.

Knowing when you are using it

You are likely to be using this process if you notice that strategy at your organisation consists of a broad strategic direction and opportunistic strategic initiatives with brief and rapidly closing windows of opportunity. If your organisation is using this process, it may even seem as though it does not have a strategy and pursues ad hoc initiatives or projects. In such situations, your organisation may begin many initiatives and abandon most of them part way through in favour of more promising ones. Usually the strategic direction or vision may reside in the minds of the strategic leader or strategic leadership team and not be explicitly articulated or communicated. But it is likely that this implicit vision is driving the recognition and pursuit of strategic opportunities. The incomplete but abandoned initiatives or projects represent initiatives that were promising opportunities at a point in time but have been eclipsed by strategic opportunities judged to be of greater benefit to the firm. If you spot many of the issues we've just discussed, it is likely that your organisation is using the Learning on the Run Process.

Process strengths and shortcomings

There are four key strengths of the Learning on the Run Process. The first is the low degree of formal structure or limited constraints on action. Low structure has been shown to enable more improvisation and experimentation, both of which are essential to the formation and realisation of emergent strategy. Second, the process enables near real-time strategy refresh, as each attempted strategic initiative essentially results in reflection and learning from intended and unintended outcomes and triggers updating of the strategic direction and in-flight strategic initiative portfolio (strategy refresh refers to the rate at which an organisation's strategy is updated to reflect changes in the internal and external environment so as to maintain relevance). An organisation's strategy might lose relevance because external environmental changes may render the strategy obsolete part way through implementation; yet, resources may remain committed and thus wasted. Achieving near real-time strategy refresh is essential in rapidly changing environments; and lack of it may risk some organisations' survival. Third, the Learning on the Run Process is simple as far as most strategy processes go. It does not contain complex language, structures or routines and is likely to be easily understood by non-strategists. Finally, this process enables anyone to make an almost immediate start on strategy execution, using the knowledge they have about the business and the environment and regardless of whether they have a clearly articulated strategy or not. This is an important strength in environments where surviving and thriving is dependent on continuous motion.

We found some shortcomings of the Learning on the Run Process. First, maintaining strategic alignment may be difficult with this process – especially if strategic direction is not well communicated and potential strategic initiatives are not vetted for fit. With similar processes, such as the Simple Rules Process, there is inbuilt alignment encapsulated in the rules themselves, but with the Learning on the Run Process, only the direction and selection of strategic opportunities shapes such alignment. As such, alignment may be difficult to maintain if the strategic direction is too broad and if there isn't adequate selection of strategic opportunities or a robust review process. Second, loosening of managerial control to drive realisation of deliberate strategy may result in diminished ability to realise such strategy in some settings. For example, in large and complex organisations that are subject to intense performance pressures, the Learning on the Run Process may be difficult to depend on to consistently satisfy those performance pressures. But this is not to say that the process can't be used in conjunction with other processes to mitigate these shortcomings. Finally, there is potential to waste significant yet scarce resources on initiatives that end up being irrelevant as conditions change. While the decision to kill off such initiatives early would be more beneficial than keeping them going, the cost associated with them may have been much less had they not been pursued in the first place.

Common tips and traps

The common traps associated with this process largely arise from its shortcomings, that is, the difficulty in creating alignment, uncertainty regarding deliberate strategy realisation and potential resource wastage. To mitigate the risks associated with the alignment challenge, we suggest that strategic leaders continuously work on improving the strategic direction to make it more specific and clear to help identify better aligned strategic opportunities. To mitigate the risks associated with uncertainty regarding deliberate strategy realisation, we suggest that strategic leaders operate this process in parallel with one or more strategy execution processes with strengths in deliberate strategy realisation. For example, the Learning on the Run Process could be operated in parallel with one of the project management processes. Or it could be operated in parallel with activity three from the Simple Rules Process: "Effect simple rules". In this case, simple rules could be put into effect to curate strategic opportunities. To mitigate the risks associated with resource wastage, we suggest that strategic leaders invest time and resources in regular review, feedback and learning to continuously update the strategic opportunities being pursued. Having done this, we advise that they then ensure the timely reallocation of resources away from obsolete strategic initiatives towards more fertile opportunities.

Spotlight on the role of strategic leaders

Strategic leaders need to discharge their fundamental role of maximising their organisation's performance and longevity. A key way they do this is by ensuring the realisation of strategies that balance the efficient pursuit of today's opportunities and mitigation of today's threats whilst building capacity to adapt to tomorrow's opportunities and threats. As you may have noticed, the key activities strategic leaders need to focus on may change depending on the strategy execution processes an organisation uses. For organisations using the Learning on the Run process, there are four essential strategic leadership activities. The first is the ongoing work to improve the clarity and specificity of the organisation's strategic direction. This is an important task since it has a strong influence on what strategic opportunities are identified, pursued and ultimately realised. An ambiguous strategic direction is likely to result in the identification and pursuit of ambiguous or irrelevant strategic opportunities that may waste scarce resources and result in greater survival risk. Second, strategic leaders need to undertake the daily work of curating strategic opportunities to identify those worth committing resources to and the timing of such resource commitments. Without this, the organisation may overcommit its resources to irrelevant strategic opportunities and find itself lacking adequate resources to pursue high-value emerging opportunities. The Learning on the Run Process is highly dependent on strategic learning to be of value. Thus, a critical third role of strategic leaders using this process is to ensure that strategic learning from intended and unintended outcomes occurs and is fed back into improvements in the strategic direction and subsequent strategic opportunities being pursued. Finally, strategic leaders need to ensure that they complement this process with activities or processes that scale up the realisation of deliberate strategies as needed.

What if you are not a strategic leader?

If you are not a strategic leader, this is another process that puts you front and centre of strategy formation and realisation. If you are able to conceive an important initiative to your organisation's future, you can make a significant contribution to your organisation's performance or positioning that will likely raise your status within the business. We suggest you begin the ongoing process of improving your strategic thinking skills,[7] improving your ability to recognise opportunities[8] and improving your ability to execute[9] on those opportunities. In Figure 9.3, we provide some examples of questions you can start reflecting on continuously.

You can discuss insights from your reflections on these questions with other people within the organisation to find potential collaborators to help further develop your ideas. Once you have developed your ideas to a certain point, you might want to consider pitching them to your line manager or to an operating manager or general manager at your organisation so as to seek sponsors that can help you further develop your ideas into prototype solutions and suggest ways to align those solutions with the organisation's strategy. While some of your

| what problems are my organization's current and potential **customers** having? |
| What new products / services or existing **product / service improvements** could solve these problems? |
| What new **product / service innovations** could be introduced in my organisation's current and potential markets? |
| What **process or technology changes** could be initiated in my organisation that could improve its efficiency and effectiveness? |
| What internal and external changes are occurring and what **opportunities or threats** are these creating for my organisation? |
| What **technological breakthroughs** should my organisation apply to improve its current product or service offerings? |
| What **new business opportunities** do recent innovations within my team or within another part of the organisation create? |

Figure 9.3 Examples of questions to continuously reflect on.

ideas may not get much traction, over time you will conceive better and better ideas, and one or more or of these ideas could turn out to be the critical bottom-up initiative that changes your organisation's destiny.

Notes

1 Welch, J., & Byrne, J. (2001). *Jack: Straight from the Gut – What I've learned leading a great company and great people*. London, England: Headline Book Publishing.
2 Leighton, A. (2008). *On leadership*. London, England: Random House.
3 Moncrieff, J. (1999), Is strategy making a difference? *Long Range Planning Review, 32*(2), 273–276.
4 Beinhocker, E. D. (1999). Robust adaptive strategies. *Sloan Management Review, 40*(3), 95.
5 Pietersen, W. (2010). Strategic learning: How to be smarter than your competition and turn key insights into competitive advantage. Hoboken, New Jersey: John Wiley & Sons.
6 Thomas, J. B., Sussman, S. W., & Henderson, J. C. (2001). Understanding "strategic learning": Linking organizational learning, knowledge management, and sensemaking. *Organization Science, 12*(3), 331–345.
7 Bowman, N. (2016, December). 4 ways to improve your strategic thinking skills. *Harvard Business Review*.
8 Grant, H. (2013, May). How to get better at spotting opportunities. *Harvard Business Review*. Retrieved from https://hbr.org/2013/05/how-to-get-better-at-spotting
9 Zenger, J., & Folkman, J. (2016, May). 4 ways to be more effective at execution. *Harvard Business Review*. Retrieved from https://hbr.org/2016/05/4-ways-to-be-more-effective-at-execution

10 The Talent Scouting Process

Origin and design principles

Origin

The Talent Scouting or Talent Placement Process was the second of four processes we found to be used in practice but having seemingly little mention in the academic or practitioner literature. Users of the process described the process as one of scouting the right individual to realise strategy and then giving them the autonomy, authority and resources to realise strategy. Where such an individual continues to realise strategy or maintains confidence that they can realise strategy, they are retained. But when confidence is lost in their ability to realise strategy, they are replaced. Although we did not find specific academic and practitioner literature on this process, we found ample literature suggesting that such a process might work. Such literature often explored the business value of mavericks,[1] the nature of mavericks,[2] the working or leadership styles of mavericks[3] and the effective leadership of mavericks.[4,5] Apple co-founder Steve Jobs put the rationale behind the Talent Scouting or Talent Placement Process well when he said, "It doesn't make sense to hire smart people and then tell them what to do. We hire smart people so they can tell us what to do".[6]

The problem

Sometimes organisations face extraordinary challenges such as a high-risk turnaround or the need for radical reinvention. Alternatively, they may be doing well but want extraordinary results. Such situations often require uniquely qualified talent (i.e. game-changing star performers or maverick performers). These rare people have the ideas, knowledge and skills to see invisible opportunities and to create seemingly inconceivable value from the organisation's resources. But as the research on such people has demonstrated, leading them can be a challenge – if they can be found and attracted to the organisation to begin with. The Talent Scouting or Talent Placement Process is a response to tapping into such people to realise strategy. The process focuses strategic leaders' efforts on scouting such star performers and providing them with the latitude to do things their way, while at the same time not abdicating responsibility for oversight of their activities and results. Examples of this process in action are abundant and include IBM's scouting of Lou Gerstner in 1993;[7] Apple's acquisition of NeXT – leading to the return of Steve Jobs;[8] HP's scouting of Meg Whitman; and Facebook's scouting of Sheryl Sandberg.[9] In each of these situations, the scouted star performer was given the latitude to do things their way and went on to transform the fate of their organisation.

The idea in brief

The key steps in the Talent Scouting or Talent Placement Process are: (1) scout a star performer or someone who can produce disproportionate value from the resources of the organisation, (2) provide them with the appropriate autonomy, resources and incentives, (3) monitor their performance, and (4) retain or replace them based on your confidence in their ability to continue to realise strategy. What follows is the unpacking and justification of each step based on the findings from our field interviews and questionnaire surveys with executive, middle management and front-line employees (see Figure 10.1).

Step 1: Scout a star performer who can produce disproportionate value from the resources of the organisation – The first step of this process requires identifying the potential star performer or maverick performer for your organisation, wooing them to your organisation and making them the type of offer that will keep them at your organisation for as long as they are needed. While on the face of it this may sound simple, spotting and attracting such game-changing talent can be an obscure art fraught with difficulties and common failure. Consider, for instance, how common it is for even the most esteemed corporations in the world, with all the resources at their disposal, to fail to attract the best CEOs or to hire the wrong ones.[10] Or consider that, with all their technical expertise in the new venture creation process, most venture capital firms still struggle to back the right founders.[11] Once spotted, attracting and retaining such a star performer can be a challenge, given the likely opportunities available to them. For example, Steve Jobs had to attract Apple's first non-founder CEO, John Sculley, from Pepsi.[12] This was no easy feat, given Pepsi's size and brand at the time relative to Apple's.

Step 2: Provide them with the appropriate autonomy, resources and incentives – A defining feature of star performers is

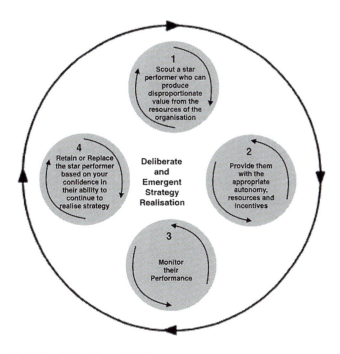

Figure 10.1 The Talent Scouting Process.

that they rarely like to be overtly led, especially by people less intelligent than them.[13] When they are led, they usually require significant autonomy. They also usually know their worth[14] and thus need to be appropriately incentivised and rewarded. Usually, incentivising and rewarding them appropriately may require thinking outside the box. Consider, for instance, the tangible and intangible incentives and rewards that the Apple board put on the table for Steve Jobs.[15] In addition to acquiring his company NeXT for a premium price, they backed him to immediately fire and replace then CEO Gil Amelio, who had undertaken the acquisition with Steve Jobs. He was able to subsequently go on and replace almost all of Apple's board. Or consider IBM's efforts to attract Lou Gerstner from American Express and risk his reputation in leading IBM, which faced very real bankruptcy prospects in 1993.[16]

Step 3: **Monitor their performance** – This step requires ongoing monitoring of the star performer's performance relative to expectations. This provides an early opportunity to determine whether the right star performer was chosen and, subsequently, the ongoing opportunity to understand the star performer's performance and its effect on the business. It also provides the opportunity to provide the star performer with feedback, should it be necessary. Performance monitoring may occur through review of financial, customer, employee and internal process measures. This may be complemented with regular conversations with the star performer regarding what initiatives they have planned, the reasons for these initiatives and the status of the initiatives.

Step 4: Retain or replace star performers based on your confidence in their ability to continue to realise strategy – This step requires that where the chosen leader is performing to expectations, or there is continued confidence in their ability to do so, their incentives and rewards are configured to retain them. These incentives and rewards may need to be amplified, for instance, if the leader's results significantly exceed expectations. Not doing so may result in star performers moving to settings where they will receive incentives and rewards more commensurate with their abilities. But where star performers underperform, or confidence is lost in their future performance, they are replaced with someone with more promising prospects.

Caveats

The Talent Scouting or Talent Placement Process steps are not episodic and sequential but always at work, even if aspects of some may have to start before others. For example, Step 1, "Scout a star performer who can produce disproportionate value from the resources of the organisation", is the ongoing daily activity of seeking out and enticing potential star performers that could transform the organisation's fortunes. The name of this process emphasises the scouting aspect of the process, which is critical, but so are all the other activities. For instance, there may not be much point to getting a star performer if the hirer cannot hold onto the star performer and get the best from them. Finally, like most other strategy execution processes, some strategy execution activities are implied. For example, learning from successes and failure and incorporating this learning into future efforts to spot, attract and lead star performers is not articulated in the process but is an essential part of the process.

What you might know it as

You may know aspects of the Talent Scouting or Talent Placement Process as part of the principles and practices of talent management. For instance, it may resemble issues addressed in talent management such as talent acquisition, onboarding, engagement and performance management. If you are from particular fields such as entertainment, professional sports or venture capital you may have a much more intimate understanding of the practice of talent scouting. Unique talent is both necessary and sufficient for successful execution. The Talent Scouting Process draws on and elaborates talent management and talent scouting practices to attract star performers who are gifted at transformation and execution and can, through force of will, personality, and talent, drive successful execution.

Prevalence

Across all sectors, we found 23 per cent of organisations, or one in every five organisations, using the Talent Scouting or Talent Placement Process to execute strategy. Usage of the Talent Scouting Process was more common across the private sector and the NGO/NFP sector, but it was also used in the public sector. The Talent Placement Process was mostly associated with high execution effectiveness in complex and chaotic environments, even though it was often used in obvious and complicated environments. Across all environments, more than half of organisations making extensive use of this process cited execution effectiveness above peers (see Figure 10.2).

The process in action

To demonstrate the Talent Scouting Process in action, we use the case study of a small events and exhibitions organisation's use of the Talent Placement Process in the Asia Pacific. The organisation is a successful family

	Sector				Employees (Org Size)				
Process	Public Sector / Government	Private Sector	NGO/NFP	All Sectors	>500	51-499	2 - 50	<2	All Sizes
7 Factor Process	10%	13%	25%	13%	19%	10%	10%	0%	12%
Execution Premium Process	24%	16%	25%	18%	25%	21%	13%	11%	18%
Simple Rules	14%	20%	17%	18%	13%	21%	23%	44%	21%
Lean Strategy Deployment Process	14%	19%	25%	18%	22%	21%	15%	11%	18%
Change Acceleration Process	14%	11%	17%	12%	9%	21%	10%	11%	12%
Project Management Process	53%	80%	66%	70%	88%	84%	63%	33%	72%
Talent Placement Process	14%	27%	25%	23%	22%	26%	23%	11%	22%
Outcomes and Incentives / Disincentives Communication Process	24%	28%	25%	26%	31%	26%	25%	11%	26%
Learning on the Run Process	39%	38%	50%	38%	31%	42%	43%	22%	37%
Resource Allocation / Portfolio Management Process	19%	17%	25%	18%	22%	21%	18%	66%	24%
Performance Monitoring and Feedback Process	39%	38%	50%	38%	44%	37%	43%	0%	38%

Figure 10.2 Proportion of study participants citing use of the Talent Scouting Process by sector and organisation size.★

Note: ★For example, of the 241 study participants, 50 participants were from the public sector/government. Of these 50 public sector/government participants, 5 participants (10%) used the 7 Factor Process. This table differs from Tables 6.23 and 6.24 shown in Busulwa (2016), where process users in each sector are shown as a proportion of all study participants. So, in the case of public sector/government users of the 7 Factor Process, this is shown as 2% (i.e. 5/241 = 2%).

business that has been established for more than 10 years, but whose owner, a serial entrepreneur, has moved on to establish firms in different industries. The case tracks his efforts to scout and manage a star CEO to operate the business and strategically take it to the next level. As you read the case, pay attention to how he approaches each step of the Talent Placement or Talent Scouting Process, as well as how he carries out the activities within that step. Also consider the organisation's unique setting, the challenges of this setting for the Talent Placement Process and how he overcomes these challenges to realise the benefits of using this process. If you believe the Talent Placement Process suits your organisation's unique setting, you may be able to adapt some of the approaches in the case study to form your organisation's unique approach to the process. Alternatively, you may decide that the process is not suited to your particular organisation – in which case one or more of the other processes in this book, or a combination of them, may be more suitable. As with other processes you may have already explored, there may be particular strategy execution insights and practices that you can pick up and adapt to whatever approach you choose to take to strategy execution.

Case study: using the Talent Scouting Process in family business – delegating the strategic leadership of an events and exhibition hire business

Colin was the owner of three businesses across the mining, event hire and exhibition and marine industries. The most profitable of these businesses was the mining business. As a result, he predominantly spent his time in the mining business, where he was heavily involved in managing operations and winning large contracts. He liked to spend any spare time on the marine business, a distributor of high-end yachts, as this fit his lifestyle interests at the time. Colin recognised the potential of the event hire and exhibition business and therefore did not want to sell it. But he lacked the time to be involved in its operations. At the same time, he recognised that good leadership was needed to ensure that its clients, many of whom were large corporations engaging the business for their corporate events, weren't disappointed. He also wanted to keep the business long enough for his children to grow up and be able to take it over. Through his business networks, Colin sought out recommendations for the best CEO to manage his event hire and exhibition business, which at the time turned over just under $4 million. The best of these recommendations, Trevor, was a senior manager at a multinational management consulting firm. But Colin wondered why Trevor would ever be interested in leaving a professional environment to roll up his sleeves and get his hands dirty, doing the hands-on execution work that would be required to develop the event hire and execution business. Colin also felt somewhat threatened as he looked further into Trevor's background and wondered whether Trevor might look down on him and his professional management shortcomings. But on the other hand, he felt that he would be able to sleep well at night with Trevor at the helm and that it would be a great opportunity to professionalise the management of the business and to better engage some of the potential corporate clients with multibillion-dollar budgets.

After speaking with some of his advisers, who advised him hiring Trevor would be a great idea if he could pull it off, Colin decided to pursue him. He started an elaborate campaign that began with seeking all the information he could about Trevor from those who had recommended him: his work interests and aspirations, his existing frustrations, his salary expectations. Colin also sourced and went through some of the different strategic reviews that Trevor had undertaken to try and understand his way of thinking. Through mutual contacts, he got word to Trevor that he was interested in discussing the condition of his business with him and an initial meeting was set. Colin did not pitch the potential CEO gig immediately but focused on forming an ongoing relationship with Trevor. Having the event and exhibition business, the marine business and the mining business meant Colin had access to a lot of high-profile circles and events. He made sure to always offer Trevor an invitation and to make Trevor the focus of his attention at these events. When he went out sailing, he made a point to invite Trevor and his family, even if they couldn't always come. He referred new business to Trevor and attended business events organised by Trevor. Over a 6-month period, in which Colin had functional manager act up as general manager of the business, Colin was able to build a good relationship with Trevor and find out that he had aspirations to be CEO and wanted to broaden his experience as an operating manager. At this point, Colin was able to make Trevor an offer he couldn't refuse. This included an annual salary that was double his existing salary (most of the firm's existing profits), profit share opportunity, a promise of full autonomy and resources to do things his way as he pursued opportunities to grow the business. Colin suggested that Trevor would have the opportunity to test all his management ideas and that irrespective of how things went, he would have invaluable experience to run a bigger firm – assuming he did not transform the event hire and exhibition business into such a firm. The opportunity eventually became too good for Trevor to forego and he agreed to take up Colin's offer. Given the nature of the business, he saw that he could continue to work with a similar client base that he had always worked with and could pull in additional professional management to help improve efficiency. Cherishing his new-found autonomy to do things his way, Trevor undertook a comprehensive review of the business' external and internal environment and devised a range of strategies aimed at transforming the event hire business into the dominant business in its industry. As part of this review, Trevor identified the firm's top three competitors within the corporate and consumer markets. With his experience in mergers and acquisitions, he was able to acquire these firms and integrate them into the existing business within the first 2 years. This significantly increased the size of the firm in a very short period of time. He was able to professionalise the firm's professional services functions to be able to attract talented professional managers. Having done this, he set about restructuring internal processes to make significant efficiency improvements. Trevor had trained as a chartered accountant and worked in investment banking, so he was able to work effectively with financiers to have all the capital he needed at his disposal. Having bolstered the size of the firm and its credibility, he set about winning over larger corporate clients nationwide.

Throughout the business' evolution, Colin's review of Trevor's performance was composed of monthly reviews of financial results and discussions of key strategic initiatives Trevor was undertaking. Colin had assembled an advisory board for this process that included esteemed business people that Trevor respected. Colin also undertook informal discussions with the business' employees, customers and other stakeholders at key company functions. Having agreed to a profit share structure, Trevor's compensation grew with his performance. But Colin complemented this with intangible rewards such as ensuring the business results were entered into key growth, quality, innovation and workplace culture competitions and that as the awards came in, Trevor got the external recognition for the business' performance.

After almost 5 years, Colin noticed Trevor start to get bored with the management of the business. Through the review process and discussions, Colin established that Trevor was ready to move onto a bigger challenge. He started to put feelers out for the company's next star performer.

Are you in the right environment for this process?

We found the Talent Scouting Process to be most used in private sector companies and in obvious and complicated environments. But irrespective of the sector or environment it was used in, most users cited execution effectiveness similar to peers (32% of users) or better than peers (64% of users). It was cited to be most effective in complex and chaotic environments. Whether this process works for you may depend on your role within the organisation. We found this particular process most used by business owners, board members and political leaders.

Knowing when you are using it

You are likely to be using this process if realising your business goals consists of finding the best talent and giving them full discretion to form and realise strategies to achieve those goals. If you find that a majority of your time is spent on spotting, enticing and attempting to hold onto such talent, then you are likely to be using this process to some degree; even though it may be complemented by other processes to plug some of its shortcomings. For instance, many boards of directors use this process to some degree to attract, incentivise and reward and monitor the performance of CEOs. But then the CEO may use a different process to realise the company's strategy. Thus, for most organisations, this process may be more and more likely to be in use at higher levels of the organisation where there is more scope for autonomy.

Process strengths and shortcomings

The greatest strength of this process lies in its potential to tap into the power of gifted people to deliver extraordinary results well beyond the capability of the ordinary talent. For instance, imagine if you are the owner of an early stage software company and you manage to pull off the seemingly impossible and hire and hold onto Steve Jobs or Bill Gates to run your company. You might be able to realise results beyond what you can possibly conceive. Other strengths of this process include its strengths at realising emergent strategy and its amenability to being operated in parallel with other strategy processes. As we've previously discussed, operating the process in parallel with other processes provides the opportunity to effect the level of ambidexterity necessary to make the most of today's business opportunities while at the same time capitalising on tomorrow's opportunities.

Potential shortcomings of the process include the extraordinary level of autonomy often required by these leaders and the risks that come with such autonomy. Providing such autonomy to the wrong person can result in catastrophic consequences to an organisation, including deep cultural and long term performance damage. For example, provision of such autonomy to former Enron CEO Jeffrey Skilling resulted in Enron's spectacular collapse. It is for this reason that the performance monitoring activity within this process is essential. It provides the opportunity to see the early signals that the wrong leader has been chosen. But this risk can remain even if the chosen leader does well initially. In such situations, there is the potential for abdication of oversight due to good past results and this abdication of oversight can lead to catastrophic setbacks.[17] For instance, such abdication may initially begin as taking performance monitoring shortcuts or not having a rigorous enough performance monitoring process (i.e. irregular or non-existent performance monitoring). In other words, autonomy should not come without accountability. Without effective oversight and clear consequences for non-performance or unacceptable risks, results can be disastrous.

Common tips and traps

The more extraordinary a star performer you are pursuing, the more extraordinary the lengths you may have to go to scout and entice such a star performer. Consider the lengths that the best talent scouts go to in fields such as professional sports, entertainment and venture capital. We also recommend taking great care to get the hiring decision right; spotting, attracting and incentivising star performers is a difficult judgement call and not an easy one at that.[18] We suggest that you be sure not to abdicate the performance monitoring part of the process, whether you feel intimidated undertaking it or find yourself too busy. You may have to get creative with how you undertake performance monitoring to be able to draw information from a range of sources without offending the star performer. Finally, we recommend that a set and forget approach is not taken with this process, but that users remain vigilant to the star performer's wants and needs, or they may become frustrated and get wooed away by competitors.

Spotlight on the role of strategic leaders

In contrast to most strategy execution processes, almost all of the steps and activities of the Talent Scouting Process are carried out or facilitated by strategic leaders. That is, without hands-on strategic leadership, this process is unlikely to be effective. Strategic leaders need to ensure that the best expertise is brought to bear to scout, attract, incentivise and reward star performers. They then need to ensure they devote time to ensuring that effective performance monitoring of the star performer's efforts is undertaken regularly to both mitigate the risks of providing so much autonomy and to enable recalibration of incentives and rewards. Finally, strategic leaders need to ensure that they are vigilant to spot the right time for a change of leadership and to bring in the next star performer that can take the organisation to the next level.

What if you are not a strategic leader?

If you are not a strategic leader and notice your organisation using this process, one of the best ways you can contribute to the strategy is to do your best to support the star leader. Such a leader may recognise your extraordinary efforts and elevate you into a high position of responsibility. They may then invest time coaching and mentoring you along the way to improve your capabilities. You may be able to repeat this process with the next star leader to be elevated to an even higher position of responsibility. With time, promotions and experience, you may be able to catch the attention of the board or business owners as a potential star leader yourself.

Notes

1 Day, G. S., & Schoemaker, P. J. (2008). Are you a 'vigilant Leader'? *MIT Sloan Management Review, 49*(3), 43.
2 Gardiner, E., & Jackson, C. J. (2012). Workplace mavericks: How personality and risk-taking propensity predicts maverickism. *British Journal of Psychology, 103*(4), 497–519.
3 Taylor, W., & LaBarre, P. G. (2006). *Mavericks at work.* New York, NY: HarperCollins Publishers.

4 Goffee, R., & Jones, G. (2007). Leading clever people. *Harvard Business Review, 85*(3), 72.

5 Goffee, R., & Jones, G. (2009). *Clever: Leading your smartest, most creative people.* Boston, MA: Harvard Business Press.

6 Beahm, G. (2011). *I, Steve: Steve Jobs in his own words.* Chicago, IL: Agate.

7 Gerstner Jr, L. V. (2009). *Who says elephants can't dance? Leading a great enterprise through dramatic change.* Grand Rapids, MI: Zondervan.

8 Isaacson, W. (2011). *Steve Jobs.* New York, NY: Simon & Schuster.

9 Auletta, K. (2012). A woman's place: Can Sheryl Sandberg upend Silicon Valley's male-dominated culture? *The New Yorker,* Retrieved from https://www.newyorker.com/magazine/2011/07/11/a-womans-place-ken-auletta

10 Charan, R. (2016). The secrets of great CEO selection. *Harvard Business Review, 94*(12), 52–59.

11 Manigart, S., Baeyens, K., & Van Hyfte, W. (2002). The survival of venture capital backed companies. *Venture capital: An International Journal of Entrepreneurial Finance, 4*(2), 103–124.

12 Isaacson, W. (2011). *Steve Jobs.* New York, NY: Simon & Schuster.

13 Taylor, W., & LaBarre, P. G. (2006). *Mavericks at work.* New York, NY: HarperCollins Publishers.

14 Goffee, R., & Jones, G. (2007). Leading clever people. *Harvard Business Review, 85*(3), 72.

15 Isaacson, W. (2011). *Steve jobs.* New York, NY: Simon & Schuster.

16 Gerstner Jr, L. V. (2009). *Who says elephants can't dance? Leading a great enterprise through dramatic change.* Grand Rapids, MI: Zondervan.

17 Kramer, R. M. (2003, October). The harder they fall. *Harvard Business Review, 81*(10), 58–68.

18 Anders, G. (2009, March). The secrets of the talent scouts. *The New York Times.* Retrieved from https://www.nytimes.com/2009/03/15/business/15talent.html

11 The Outcomes and Incentives Communication Process

Origin and design principles

Origin

The Outcomes and Incentives Communication Process was the third of four processes we found to be used in practice but having little mention in the academic or practitioner literature. Users of the process described it as one of communicating desired outcomes and communicating the incentives or disincentives for achievement of these outcomes. For example, X-Prize operates incentivised public competitions, such as the $20 million Lunar X-Prize,[1] to encourage particular technological developments for the benefit of humanity. This process may perhaps best be conceptualised by the "Wanted: Reward" notices issued by policing, investigation and intelligence agencies to assist in the capture of fugitives.[2] In such notices, a desired outcome is communicated (e.g. the capture of the fugitive or provision of information leading to the capture of the fugitive). The corresponding reward for delivering on the desired outcome is communicated (e.g. monetary reward). We did not find specific academic and practitioner literature on this process, but we found ample literature suggesting that such a process might work in practice. This literature mostly described the effect of different types of incentives on the behaviours of groups of people within or outside of an organisation. Examples of this literature included organisation-wide performance management through rewards,[3] rewards-based performance management of CEOs[4] and executives,[5,6] incentives-based management of middle management,[7] team,[8] front-line employee[9] and business co-founder behaviours.[10]

The problem

In the case of law enforcement agencies seeking fugitives, for example, they are usually clear on who has to be captured but lack the necessary information or know-how to capture a fugitive. In such situations, they broadcast the desired outcomes widely and offer large incentives to motivate anyone out there with the knowledge or capabilities to take the actions necessary for law enforcement agencies to realise their desired outcomes. Similarly, in strategy execution, there may be times when the desired strategic outcomes are clear, but it is unclear who has the know-how to realise them. The Outcomes and Incentives Communication Process is a solution to the challenges of such situations. It prescribes communication of the desired strategic outcomes as well as the incentives to be given to anyone realising such outcomes. In doing so, it enables motivation of those with the know-how and motivation to execute desired strategic outcomes in order to acquire the corresponding incentives. Whereas with law enforcement use of this process, the incentives have mostly been financial, in an organisation context, the rewards can be a combination of tangible and intangible incentives.

The idea in brief

The key steps in the Outcomes and Incentives Communication Process are as follows: (1) determine desired strategic outcomes, (2) determine the incentives likely to motivate realisation of strategic outcomes, (3) communicate the strategic outcomes, incentives and disincentives and (4) learn from intended and unintended results. What follows is the unpacking and justification of each step based on the findings from our field interviews and questionnaire surveys with executive, middle management and front-line employees (Figure 11.1).

Step 1: Determine desired strategic outcomes – The first step of this process is to identify the desired strategic outcomes. Identifying the best outcomes requires that strategic leaders have gotten an intimate understanding of their internal and external environment, and subsequently, the immediate, medium and long-term opportunities and threats for their organisation. Having done this, they can then identify the critical three or four desired strategic outcomes that will maximise their organisation's profitability and/or longevity. These desired strategic outcomes then need to be translated into the format that will be most understandable, compelling and memorable for the target audience.

Step 2: Determine affordable incentives and disincentives most likely to motivate realisation of strategic outcomes – Once the critical desired strategic outcomes are identified, Step 2 requires determining what incentives are necessary to motivate their realisation

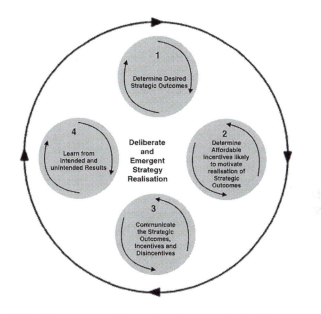

Figure 11.1 The Outcomes and Incentives Communication Process.

and what disincentives are necessary to discourage risky behaviours that may be undertaken in the pursuit of the strategic outcomes. Think of disincentives as penalties for violating the rules of a sporting game. If such rules are violated, then the athlete may be disqualified from winning the prize, for example. And, continuing with the sports analogy, the incentives can be thought of as the tangible and intangible rewards of winning. For example, these could include prize money, fame and sponsorship opportunities. An important caveat is that the incentives as well as the enforcement of disincentives both have to be affordable and desirable.

Step 3: Communicate the strategic outcomes, incentives and disincentives – Once the strategic outcomes and the incentives and disincentives to drive their safe achievement are clear, Step 3 requires that these are communicated to the target audience. Strategic leaders can use the most effective modes of communication for their particular environment. For example, communication may be top-down or bottom-up, formal or informal, internal or external, one-time or in continuous mode, lateral or not lateral, digital or face-to-face. It can occur through meetings, emails, newsletters, town hall forums, websites, posters and offsite sessions.

Step 4: Learn from intended and unintended results – In this final step, strategic leaders pay attention to the outcomes and learn from the incentives and disincentives that are working and not working. This enables them to iteratively improve the activities within each of the earlier steps discussed, even if they do not find immediate success in using the process.

Caveats

As with other processes, the Outcomes and Incentives Communication Process steps are not episodic and sequential but always at work, even if aspects of some may have to start before others. The activities within the four steps and the ongoing updating of the outcomes of those activities are the daily responsibility of strategic leaders. The iterative nature of the process enables the real-time updating of the organisation's desired strategic outcomes, of the incentives used to drive realisation of those outcomes, of the disincentives used to mitigate risks associated with the pursuit of those outcomes and, finally, of the optimisation of communication and learning efforts.

What you might know it as

The concept of using incentives to motivate behaviours is an accepted idea. Its application to strategy execution in this format is novel. If you are familiar with the research and practitioner literature on the use of incentives to motivate particular behaviours, you may find the Outcomes and Incentives Communication Process to have some similarities with these theories and practices. Examples of such research and practitioner literature includes those looking at the use and effectiveness of different reward management systems,[11] those looking at the use and effectiveness of different forms of compensation[12] and those looking at effective compensation for different employee groups.[13,14]

Prevalence

Across all sectors, we found 26 per cent of organisations, or one in every five organisations, using the Outcomes and Incentives Communication Process to execute strategy. The process was mostly used in the private sector and was used twice as much in large and small businesses as in medium-sized organisations. About half of process users cited execution effectiveness above their peers and approximately half of users cited execution effectiveness to be same as their peers. The process

Process	Sector				Employees (Org Size)				
	Public Sector / Government	Private Sector	NGO/NFP	All Sectors	>500	51-499	2 - 50	<2	All Sizes
7 Factor Process	10%	13%	25%	13%	19%	10%	10%	0%	12%
Execution Premium Process	24%	16%	25%	18%	25%	21%	13%	11%	18%
Simple Rules	14%	20%	17%	18%	13%	21%	23%	44%	21%
Lean Strategy Deployment Process	14%	19%	25%	18%	22%	21%	15%	11%	18%
Change Acceleration Process	14%	11%	17%	12%	9%	21%	10%	11%	12%
Project Management Process	53%	80%	66%	70%	88%	84%	63%	33%	72%
Talent Placement Process	14%	27%	25%	23%	22%	26%	23%	11%	22%
Outcomes and Incentives / Disincentives Communication Process	24%	26%	25%	26%	31%	26%	25%	11%	26%
Learning on the Run Process	39%	38%	50%	38%	31%	42%	43%	22%	37%
Resource Allocation / Portfolio Management Process	19%	17%	25%	18%	22%	21%	18%	66%	24%
Performance Monitoring and Feedback Process	39%	38%	50%	38%	44%	37%	43%	0%	38%

Figure 11.2 Proportion of study participants citing use of the Outcomes and Incentives Communication Process by sector and organisation size.*

Note: *For example, of the 241 study participants, 50 participants were from the public sector/government. Of these 50 public sector/government participants, 5 participants (10%) used the 7 Factor Process. This table differs from Tables 6.23 and 6.24 shown in Busulwa (2016), where process users in each sector are shown as a proportion of all study participants. So, in the case of public sector/government users of the 7 Factor Process, this is shown as 2% (i.e. 5/241 = 2%).

was mostly associated with high execution effectiveness in complex and chaotic environments, even though it was used more in obvious and complicated environments (see Figure 11.2).

The process in action

To demonstrate the Outcomes and Incentives Communication Process in action, we use the case study of the Ventura County Sheriff's department and its efforts to capture a wealthy fugitive who had escaped from the United States and was outside of the department's jurisdiction.[15] While the case study demonstrates the use of the process to communicate outcomes and incentives to an audience outside of the department's staff, we chose it for how well it demonstrates the process in action as well as how well it demonstrates the process' strengths and weaknesses. As you review the case, consider the strengths and shortcomings of the process. Also consider the Ventura County Sheriff's department's unique setting and the potential challenges of this setting for the Outcomes and Incentives Communication Process. If you believe the process suits your organisation's unique setting, you may be able to adapt some of the approaches in the case study to form your organisation's unique approach to the process. But you might also decide that the process is not suited to your particular organisation – in which case one or more of the other processes in this book, or a combination of them, may be more suitable. Still, there may be particular strategy execution insights and practices that you can pick up and adapt to whatever approach you choose to take to strategy execution.

Case study: the Ventura County Sheriff's Department – using the Outcomes and Incentives Communication Process to apprehend a fugitive outside the country

In 2000, Andrew Luster, the great grandson of cosmetics giant Max Factor and heir to the Max Factor cosmetics fortune, was arrested by the Ventura County Sheriff's department and charged with drugging and sexually assaulting three women. His bail was set at $1 million. Although his bail was posted, he was reported to have escaped and left the country under a false identity. "He's gone", Gary Auer, the chief investigator for the Ventura County district attorney's office, had confirmed. "He has a lot of money and extensive contacts around the world", Gary added.[16] After extensive but uneventful efforts, the department decided it needed to work with the FBI and to cast a wide local and international net, as well as to incentivise action outside of the department's staff. Receiving information on his whereabouts was not likely to be enough given jurisdiction limitations. Being clear on its desired outcome (the capture of Andrew Luster), the search team decided to offer a share of his forfeited $1 million bail of up to $150,000 for his capture. The search team started to communicate the desired outcome and incentive far and wide, using a range of different communication mediums including online and television media channels.

News of his desired capture and the size of the associated reward attracted widespread international attention. Self-described bounty hunters Duane "Dog" Chapman and his wife were some of the many people the communication reached, and they became consumed with hunting down the fugitive in the hopes of collecting the $150,000 reward. Using their own resources, they began a comprehensive search for any information on Andrew Luster. As part of their search, they sought out different media outlets. "We've been researching him. We have ate, slept and drank this person for six months. I've hardly seen my husband. He missed Valentine's Day, Mother's Day, Father's Day", Duane's wife and partner said on *Good Morning America*. In their search, Duane and his wife assembled a scrapbook of information on the fugitive, including information from police, Luster's victims, and others, including his cosmetic surgeons. Their search was extensive and included appearances on television discussing the case. Their hard work eventually paid off when they received an anonymous tip from a young woman returning on vacation from Mexico who told them, "Hey, I think I partied with that guy!". Once they verified the information, Duane Chapman got onto a plane to Mexico. Once there, he used a range of means to track Luster down in Mexico, and on an open street, using pepper spray, he seized Luster in front of a group of surprised bystanders. The bystanders called Mexican police, who, unable to sort out who was who, arrested both Chapman and Luster.[17]

On review of the case of the arrested men, Mexican authorities ordered Luster deported to the United States. FBI agents escorted Luster back to the Ventura County Sheriff's department to serve the 124-year prison sentence he had received in absentia.[18] Although Ventura County and the FBI got their fugitive, Duane and his wife did not get their reward or incentive in the end.[19] In their pursuit of Luster, Duane had broken a number of Mexican laws, including illegally entering Mexico and bounty hunting in the country, which is an illegal offence there. Duane faced charges by Mexican authorities for these illegal acts, and after a difficult legal battle, he was lucky to win extradition to the United States. Ventura County Superior Court Judge Edward Brodie awarded the $150,000 to Ventura County instead, saying, "I don't condone vigilante justice that violates the law". Ventura County used the Outcomes and Incentives Communication Process to get their fugitive, but because they did not communicate some important disincentives, a number of important laws were broken, and this diminished the value they realised from the process.

Are you in the right environment for this process?

We found use of the Outcomes and Incentives Communication Process to be most commonly used in the private sector. Use of this process was about the same across obvious, complex, chaotic and high-velocity/high-volatility environments. But although it could be effective in most environments, it was most often associated with high and very high execution effectiveness in complex and chaotic environments. Thus, if you are in such settings, then this process may be right for you. However, use of this process requires that you are also in a position to issue incentives, to enforce disincentives and to effectively communicate to the target audience. Further, it is worth considering any risks that your organisation might face through use of this process and the organisation's capacity to mitigate or absorb these risks. For example, the Ventura County could have anticipated some of the risks in the Luster case and communicated disincentives to discourage such behaviours.

Knowing when you are using it

You are likely to be using the Outcomes and Incentives Communication Process if the four steps described earlier resemble the steps taken by your organisation to execute strategy. Most organisations will likely be using this process to some degree, though it may be more focused on operational or routine performance outcomes than strategic outcomes. For example, it may be used to achieve outcomes such as appropriate employee behaviours and performance. In such situations, the desired outcomes and incentives may be implicitly understood. For example, outcomes and incentives such as "adhere to organisation values" and "deliver on expectations" to "remain employed here" or "get promoted" are implicitly in place at most organisations. But at other organisations, such outcomes and incentives may be deliberately crafted to drive strategy realisation. Your organisation may be somewhere along the continuum between unconscious use of the process to realise operational outcomes and deliberate use of the process to drive strategy realisation.

Process strengths and shortcomings

The first key strength of the Outcomes and Incentives Communication Process is its ability to push opportunity recognition, on-the-spot decision-making and improvisatory action to teams within the organisation or outside of the organisation. In doing so, the process enables people and teams across the organisation and outside it to adapt to rapidly changing local circumstances and to seize fleeting opportunities in near to real time. For example, the Ventura County Police department was able to tap into and engage people outside of the department to pursue its desired outcomes. This strength is unique to this process, as most other processes constrain strategic action to teams within the organisation. Another related strength of the process is its ability to surface invisible strategy execution talent and invisible approaches to strategy execution. For example, the Ventura County Police department may have had little knowledge that a team like Duane and his wife would be out there and the department may have learned valuable lessons from the actions Duane and his wife took to apprehend Luster. Without providing the autonomy inherent in the Outcomes and Incentives Communication Process, the department may not have learned about Duane and his wife or of the additional approaches to apprehending fugitives that Duane and his wife enlightened them to. Another key strength of this process is that it is very easy to use it in parallel with other processes and it may complement such processes very well. For example, some organisations may use this process for innovation tournaments to achieve additional innovation outcomes outside of their conventional strategy execution process.

There are three key shortcomings of this process that stuck out. The first and most significant is the potential risks that could emanate from the autonomous actions of those incentivised to action. For instance, in the Luster case, Duane's actions may have created unnecessary risk for US/Mexico relations or resulted in Duane being imprisoned or even losing his life. None of these things would have reflected well on the Ventura County Police department's leadership. Given the laws that Duane broke, Judge Brodie chose not to create a potentially dangerous precedent by awarding Duane the $150,000 reward. It's true that the Ventura County Police department could have incorporated tighter disincentives in their campaign such as "breaking any local or international laws invalidates the reward and may result in prosecution". But still, some necessary disincentives are difficult to anticipate prospectively. A second shortcoming of the process is that it may be difficult to know whether strategy execution is actually happening or, if it is happening, what progress has been made. This is mainly because people potentially pursuing the reward and thus undertaking strategy execution may not come forward until they have achieved the outcomes and can collect the reward. Finally, this process may be strongly oriented towards the achievement of deliberate strategy, even though this is done through autonomous action. But this is dependent on how tightly desired outcomes and incentives are defined. For example, if the desired strategic actions are "find a new healthcare product offering and achieve $150 million revenue this financial year", this desired outcome may enable a combination of deliberate and emergent strategy realisation. But, if the desired strategic action is "sell 10 per cent more of product B", then the potential for emergent strategy realisation may be reduced.

Common tips and traps

We anticipate that the most challenging part of this process is the potential risk from the autonomous actions of those taking action in pursuit of the rewards. There may be no limit to the surprising actions people choose to take and the potential negative effects of these actions. In Duane's case, he broke international laws and put his life at risk. Because of this, we suggest that significant care is taken in choosing the desired strategic outcomes and the corresponding incentives and the disincentives. Serious thought should be given to the types of positive and negative behaviours and actions that are likely to be encouraged and discouraged and the potential risks inherent in such behaviours. We suggest that care is also taken in how tightly desired strategic outcomes, incentives and disincentives are defined to enable the appropriate level of deliberate and emergent strategy to be realised. If defined too tightly, then the realisation of emergent strategy is constrained, but if defined too loosely, then deliberate strategy realisation is constrained. An alternative approach to striking the right balance may be to focus this process on the realisation of a particular type of strategy and use a different process in parallel to realise the other type of strategy. For example, the Outcomes and Incentives Communication Process may be configured for the efficient realisation of emergent strategy while the Execution Premium Process is configured to optimise the realisation of deliberate strategy. If you are using this process, it is important to deliver the promised rewards – it may even be more beneficial to over-deliver. The more certain prospective action takers are that they will receive the promised rewards, the more engaged they will be and the faster your desired outcomes may be achieved. Finally, if you are using this process, we suggest that you begin small and expand your efforts gradually as you learn from trial and error and from the resultant intended and unintended consequences of using the process in your setting.

Spotlight on the role of strategic leaders

To discharge their fundamental role of ensuring the realisation of strategies that achieve an optimal balance between efficiency and adaptation, this process requires hands-on strategic leadership involvement. Specifically, strategic leaders need to ensure that the most important strategic objectives are identified, prioritised and translated into a clearly understandable format, that is, that these strategic objectives are translated into unambiguous desired strategic outcomes. Strategic leaders then have to have a process in place that ensures that great care is taken to devise the right incentives and disincentives to drive the pursuit of desired strategic outcomes in a safe manner. They then need to ensure that earned incentives are issued and that disincentives are enforced. In addition to all this, strategic leaders need to remain vigilant at all times to potential risks emanating from autonomous actions being taken in the pursuit of desired outcomes as well as lessons to learn and use to update current and future outcomes, incentives and disincentives. All these responsibilities are ongoing, day in and day out tasks of strategic leaders using this process. The efficiency and effectiveness with which strategic leaders carry out these tasks determines the efficiency and effectiveness with which the organisation realises its desired deliberate and emergent strategy. As we have discussed earlier, the efficiency and effectiveness with which an organisation realises deliberate and emergent strategies ultimately determines its fate.

What if you are not a strategic leader?

In this process, strategic leaders simply communicate the desired strategic outcomes and leave you to consider and act on the action plans that will achieve these strategies the quickest. If your organisation uses this process, we suggest that you continuously develop your ability to form action plans and to execute these plans faster than others. This way, when desired strategic outcomes are communicated, you can improve your odds of being the first to deliver on these outcomes and get the incentives or rewards. Building your capacity to form and execute action plans may require you to continuously improve your ability to think strategically and to follow through on your planned actions. It is also likely to require you to continuously improve your ability to engage others and motivate them to support you in the pursuit of strategic outcomes. For instance, to succeed in capturing Luster, Duane the bounty hunter had to successfully engage and motivate media channels and the general public to support his cause.

Notes

1 Sheetz, M. (2017, January). Google's $20 million race to the moon will end with no winner — and Google is OK with that. *CNBC*.
2 BBC News. (2015). US offers $3m reward for arrest of Russian hacker Evgeniy Bogachev, Retrieved September 15, 2016, from http://www.bbc.com/news/world-us-canada-31614819
3 Armstrong, M. (2010). *Armstrong's handbook of reward management practice: Improving performance through reward*. London, UK: Kogan Page Publishers.

4 Makri, M., Lane, P. J., & Gomez-Mejia, L. R. (2006). CEO incentives, innovation, and performance in technology-intensive firms: a reconciliation of outcome and behavior-based incentive schemes. *Strategic Management Journal, 27*(11), 1057–1080.

5 Guay, W., Core, J., & Larcker, D. (2003). *Executive equity compensation and incentives: A survey.* Federal Reserve Bank of New York. Retrieved from https://www.newyorkfed.org/medialibrary/media/research/epr/03v09n1/0304core.pdf

6 Guay, W., Core, J., & Larcker, D. (2003). *Executive equity compensation and incentives: A survey.* Federal Reserve Bank of New York. Retrieved from https://www.newyorkfed.org/medialibrary/media/research/epr/03v09n1/0304core.pdf

7 Baker, G. P. (1990). Pay-for-performance for middle managers: causes and consequences. *Journal of Applied Corporate Finance, 3*(3), 50–61.

8 Bandiera, O., Barankay, I., & Rasul, I. (2013). Team incentives: Evidence from a firm level experiment. *Journal of the European Economic Association, 11* (5), 1079–1114.

9 Shields, J., Brown, M., Kaine, S., Dolle-Samuel, C., North-Samardzic, A., McLean, P., … & Plimmer, G. (2015). *Managing employee performance & reward: Concepts, practices, strategies.* Cambridge: Cambridge University Press.

10 Wasserman, N., & Hellman, T. (2016, February). The very first mistake most startup founders make. *Harvard Business Review.*

11 Armstrong, M. (2010). *Armstrong's handbook of reward management practice: Improving performance through reward.* Kogan Page Publishers.

12 Guay, W., Core, J., & Larcker, D. (2002). *Executive equity compensation and incentives: A survey.*

13 Bandiera, O., Barankay, I., & Rasul, I. (2013). Team incentives: Evidence from a firm level experiment. *Journal of the European Economic Association, 11*(5), 1079–1114.

14 Baker, G. P. (1990). Pay-for-performance for middle managers: causes and consequences. *Journal of Applied Corporate Finance, 3* (3), 50–61.

15 Leduff, C (2003). Cosmetics heir is missing as his rape trial proceeds. *New York Times,* Retrieved September 15, 2015 from http://www.nytimes.com/2003/01/08/us/cosmetics-heir-is-missing-as-his-rape-trial-proceeds.html

16 Leduff, C. (2003). Cosmetics heir is missing as his rape trial proceeds. *New York Times,* Retrieved September 15, 2015, from http://www.nytimes.com/2003/01/08/us/cosmetics-heir-is-missing-as-his-rape-trial-proceeds.html

17 Francescan, C. (2003). How bounty hunters got fugitive heir. *ABC News,* Retrieved September 15, 2015, from http://abcnews.go.com/GMA/story?id=125050&page=1

18 CNN.com. (2003) Max Factor heir returns to face prison term. *CNN,* Retrieved from http://edition.cnn.com/2003/LAW/06/19/max.factor.heir/

19 Collins, D. (2003). Luster hunter can't cash in. *CBS News* Retrieved from http://www.cbsnews.com/news/luster-hunter-cant-cash-in/

12 The Performance Monitoring and Coaching Process

Origin and design principles

Origin

The Performance Monitoring and Coaching Process was the last of the four processes we found used in practice[1] but not discussed in the academic or practitioner literature. Users of the process described it as one of co-creating strategic objectives, agreeing on strategic actions to be undertaken, monitoring the effectiveness of these actions and undertaking coaching to optimise reflection, learning and future performance. While we did not find specific academic and practitioner literature on this process, there was a lot of experiential learning and performance coaching literature supporting the process. The experiential learning literature proposes that some things can only be learned through doing and reflection on doing.[2,3,4,5] This literature proposes that for such things, the learning process ought to consist of the following activities: taking action, experiencing the effects of that action, reflecting on the experience to understand cause and effect, thinking about and devising ways to improve subsequent actions and repeating this process until actions taken yield the desired outcomes.[6,7,8] In contrast, the coaching literature proposes that the achievement of personal or professional goals can be optimised through the coaching process.[9,10] In the coaching process, a coach supports a coachee's own efforts to achieve personal or business objectives by facilitating access to appropriate guidance, objective feedback, insightful reflection, accountability and resolution of obstacles.[11,12] Thus, in essence, the Performance Monitoring and Coaching Process brings together and adapts the experiential learning and coaching processes to strategy execution.

The problem

At times, people find themselves in strategic leadership roles but with little strategic leadership or strategy execution experience. Examples of such situations may be found in organisations where a great technical leader moves into a strategic leadership role or where a high potential leader is elevated into a strategic leadership role. These situations may occur deliberately on the logic that strategic leadership and strategy execution are best learned by doing. At other times, the situation may be dictated by unexpected events. For example, consider people thrust into strategic leadership roles as a result of unexpected events like crises or abrupt and unexpected leadership departures. New strategic leaders in such situations may learn strategy execution through experiential learning. But there are clearly some significant risks that arise from their lack of experience and know-how. These risks include undertaking actions or failing to take actions that may put the survival of the firm in jeopardy. The Performance Monitoring and Coaching Process mitigates some of this risk by providing a way to prospectively review intended actions, monitor the effects of those actions as they are taken and ensure that optimal reflection, learning and subsequent remedial actions occur. For example, any intended strategic actions and their intended implementation plans can be reviewed for appropriateness, modified as needed, actioned, their effects and the implications of those effects reviewed and subsequent follow-up strategic actions debated. In doing so, the risks of the wrong actions being taken, or necessary actions not being taken, can be mitigated. Similarly, the risks that may be inherent in individual approaches to implementing those actions or learning the wrong lessons from reflection can also be mitigated. In line with situational leadership prescriptions, the amount of constraint on strategic leaders' actions can be loosened over time from "telling" to "selling" to "participating" to full "delegation".[13,14] Changes in the degree of constraint on action would in turn change risk exposure for the organisation.

The idea in brief

The key steps in the Performance Monitoring and Coaching Process are as follows: (1) co-create strategic objectives, (2) agree on priority strategic actions to be undertaken, (3) encourage effecting of agreed strategic actions, (4) monitor performance effectiveness and (5) undertake coaching to optimise reflection, learning and future execution. What follows is the unpacking and justification of each step

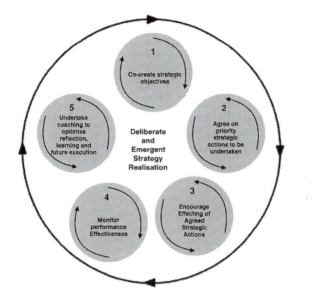

Figure 12.1 The Performance Monitoring and Coaching Process.

based on the findings from our field interviews and questionnaire surveys with executive, middle management and front-line employees (see Figure 12.1).

Step 1: Co-create strategic objectives – The first step involves forming the organisation's strategic objectives. Doing this requires that strategic leaders have gotten an intimate understanding of their internal and external environment and, subsequently, the immediate, medium and long-term opportunities and threats for their organisation. Depending on the newness of the strategic leader to strategic leadership or to the business and its context, this is usually best done as a co-creation process. That is, both the strategic leader and their overseer or coach (e.g. a member of the board of directors, an advisor, a professional coach etc.) get an intimate understanding of the business' internal and external environment and its immediate, medium and short-term opportunities and threats. Together, they can reconcile their perceptions of the environment, the opportunities and threats and the strategic objectives identified to arrive at the final priority strategic objectives for the organisation. As the strategic leader's capabilities improve with experiential learning and coaching, the overseer or coach's role may shift from having the final say with regarding what strategic objectives are pursued to simply review the strategic leader's logic and constructively challenging their logic for any blind spots or oversights.[15]

Step 2: Agree on priority strategic actions to be undertaken – Having identified the organisation's strategic objectives, Step 2 translates those objectives into specific actions with clear accountability, delivery time frames and resources. These strategic actions are then prioritised. As with the first step, this step is also jointly undertaken by the overseer or coach and the strategic leader.

Step 3: Encourage the effecting agreed actions – Once priority strategic actions are identified and resources for their achievement allocated, Step 3 requires that the strategic leader is encouraged to go off and effect the agreed actions. As a part of this process, they will usually discuss their plans for effecting the agreed actions with their overseer or coach who can ensure that the plans are constructively challenged and any potential issues with the plans are identified and modified as before action is taken. Once the overseer or coach has agreed that the strategic leader's plans are likely to work, the strategic leader can begin actioning them and tap into the coach's insights regarding any issues that might emerge during implementation.

Step 4: Monitor performance effectiveness – In this step, ongoing monitoring of the organisation's and the strategic leader's performance relative to expectations is undertaken. This provides an opportunity for immediate feedback on the effectiveness of the strategic actions being undertaken and the effectiveness of the strategic leader's approach to effecting these strategic actions. Performance information can also be used by both the coach and coachee to enhance the experiential learning and coaching processes. Performance monitoring usually occurs through review of financial, customer, employee and internal process measures. But it is best to complement it with other information sources (e.g. regular conversations with the strategic leader and with their direct reports) to understand the situation on the ground.

Step 5: Undertake coaching to optimise reflection, learning and future execution – The magic of this process largely occurs in the fifth step. In this step, the coach utilises an effective coaching approach and effective coaching skills to ensure that the strategic leader is receiving appropriate guidance, objective feedback, insightful reflection on the effects of their actions, accountability and an optimal learning environment. When these things are done well, the strategic leader will develop their strategic leadership and strategy execution capabilities at a rapid rate. They may, in turn, be better suited to replicate this coaching approach with their management team and, in turn, accelerate the realisation of strategy.

Caveats

As with other processes, the Performance Monitoring and Coaching Process steps or activities are iterative. The steps are not episodic and sequential but always at work, often in parallel. The activities of this process are the routine responsibility of strategic leaders and their overseers. This process may be used by a board chairperson, a business owner or a key shareholder to drive strategy execution via a strategic leader such as a CEO or general manager. But it could be just as easily used by any strategic leader to shape strategy execution via their direct reports, although the strategic scope may be more limited.

What you might know it as

If you are familiar with the academic and practitioner literature on experiential learning, coaching or action learning, then you will recognise that this process essentially brings together the key insights from these areas about learning from doing and optimising performance through the benefits of the coaching process. If you have undertaken general management in particular settings, it may have largely relied on a combination of experiential learning and coaching to get direct reports to buy into the organization's strategy and to align their actions in support of realising that strategy. The process essentially brings insights from those areas and applies them to the shaping of strategy execution for strategic leaders that are new to strategic leadership, new to an organisations context or can benefit from coaching.

Prevalence

We found 38 per cent of organisations, or two in every five organisations, to be using the Performance Monitoring and Coaching Process to execute strategy, although not necessarily using it in isolation from other approaches. Usage of the process was about the same across sectors, although the NGO/NFP sector was a more prominent user. Usage of the process was also the same across organisation sizes and environments. This process was mostly associated with high and very high execution effectiveness in all environments (see Figure 12.2).

| | Sector | | | | Employees (Org Size) | | | | |
Process	Public Sector / Government	Private Sector	NGO/NFP	All Sectors	>500	51-499	2 - 50	<2	All Sizes
7 Factor Process	10%	13%	25%	13%	19%	10%	10%	0%	12%
Execution Premium Process	24%	16%	25%	18%	25%	21%	13%	11%	18%
Simple Rules	14%	20%	17%	18%	13%	21%	23%	44%	21%
Lean Strategy Deployment Process	14%	19%	25%	18%	22%	21%	15%	11%	18%
Change Acceleration Process	14%	11%	17%	12%	9%	21%	10%	11%	12%
Project Management Process	53%	80%	66%	70%	88%	84%	63%	33%	72%
Talent Placement Process	14%	27%	25%	23%	22%	26%	23%	11%	22%
Outcomes and Incentives / Disincentives Communication Process	24%	28%	25%	26%	31%	26%	25%	11%	26%
Learning on the Run Process	39%	38%	50%	38%	31%	42%	43%	22%	37%
Resource Allocation / Portfolio Management Process	19%	17%	25%	18%	22%	21%	18%	66%	24%
Performance Monitoring and Feedback Process	39%	38%	50%	38%	44%	37%	43%	0%	38%

Figure 12.2 Proportion of study participants citing use of the Performance Monitoring and Coaching Process by sector and organisation size.★

The process in action

To demonstrate the Performance Monitoring and Coaching Process in action, we use the case study of a relatively early stage custom software development company, at which the company's CEO is a software developer who has been thrust into the strategic leadership role. As you review the case, consider the strengths and shortcomings of the process. Also consider the software company's unique setting and the potential challenges of this setting for the Performance Monitoring and Coaching Process as well as for other processes. If you decide the process is not for you, there may be particular strategy execution insights and practices that you can pick up and adapt to whatever approach you choose to take to strategy execution.

Case study: using the Performance Monitoring and Coaching Process to shape the strategy execution of a custom software business

Steve and Nick were the owners of a custom software development firm that provided custom cloud, IoT and mobile application development services. Steve and Nick had built the business from scratch to a point where it employed five full-time developers and turned over half a million dollars. In early 2013, Steve, as CEO, managed to attract James to help the business lay the foundations to scale. Initially, James was engaged on a part time consultancy basis but had an immediate positive impact on the software business. Observing this impact, Steve drew on all the resources at his disposal to hire James in a full-time capacity. James discussed with Steve the benefits of an advisory board and they both agreed that it would be beneficial to recruit such a team to become a sounding board to Steve. In the process of recruiting a five-member advisory board, Steve and James came across Tony, a senior lawyer who was the CEO of a Software as a Service (SAAS) company which he had managed to recently scale from $1 million to $50 million. Steve and James weren't successful in recruiting Tony to be on the advisory board but eventually succeeded in getting him on board as an investor.

Once on board as an investor, Tony set up a fortnightly management team meeting between himself, Steve, Nick and James. In the first meeting, Tony asked the management team to undertake a review of its internal and external environment as well as its immediate, medium and long-term opportunities and threats. The subsequent meeting was a lively debate between Tony and the management team regarding the company's industry, the opportunities and threats within that industry and the importance of the products and services offered by the company. The management team was astounded by Tony's understanding of the industry and the opportunities and threats facing the business. After intense debate, the team decided on a clear strategy for the company that included growing the cloud, IoT and mobile application services in particular industries, growing subscription revenue from those services, prioritising opportunities to build industry-specific software platforms that could be resold, growing turnover to $3 million that financial year and tripling the team size. Steve and the team were energised by their new-found strategic clarity.

At the end of that meeting, Tony asked the team to devise a draft Balanced Scorecard template to report on the critical business performance indicators each fortnight. When Steve presented the draft scorecard the following fortnight, Tony asked incisive questions about each indicator the team had chosen and its relevance each fortnight. The team debated the measures and discussed issues such as meaning, importance of regular review ease of reporting and ownership of reporting each measure. The team then spent much time translating the company's strategic objectives into Key Performance Indicators (KPIs) using the identified performance measures. Ownership of each KPI was then discussed. After another engaging debate, the team left with even more clarity about the strategic actions necessary to achieve the company's strategic objectives and accountability for each strategic action. Steve was delighted with the clarity that had been achieved in just a few meetings. He was a software engineer and knew how to lead small software teams to deliver on software projects but had been thrust into general management as his co-founder was a strong introvert and wanted nothing to do with it. Steve had been meandering his way through general management over the last 5 years and now realised that his limited knowledge had limited the potential of the firm.

In the proceeding fortnightly meetings, the management team settled into a process with Tony that consisted of each management team member discussing what of the previous fortnight's agreed strategic actions they had achieved and not achieved, the obstacles they had faced in the pursuit of strategic actions, what they believed they did well and needed to do better, whether they were still on track to achieve the monthly and annual strategic objectives allocated to them and what they believed their priority strategic actions for the next fortnight needed to be. The team would then review changes in the business performance scorecard and discuss the cause and effect behind it. During these discussions, Tony used the performance scorecard as a source of objective feedback on individual and business performance. He used a range of questioning approaches to constructively challenge management team members to reflect on the actions they had taken and the effects of those actions. As personal and business obstacles emerged, he drew on his experience running a similar company to provide guidance and build the confidence of Steve and his management team. Where he didn't have specific experience, he drew on his network to connect the team to this experience. Tony also made himself available to team members for any questions that emerged throughout the fortnight.

Over the course of 12 months, the management team was able to grow in confidence and execution capability to the point where it started to significantly exceed the strategic objectives set at the start of the year. For example, while a stretch revenue target of $3 million was set, the team won and delivered on some large contracts near the end of the year that saw it achieve

$5 million annual revenue. At the end of the 12-month period, one of the customers for whom it had delivered a large mobile application approached the company with a large acquisition offer. At the time of writing this case, the company was still considering whether to take this offer or whether to continue along its recent growth trajectory.

Are you in the right environment for this process?

We found the Performance Monitoring and Coaching Process to have similar usage level and effectiveness across sectors, organisation sizes and environments. Irrespective of where it was used, most users cited high to very high strategy execution effectiveness. Therefore, this process is likely to be appropriate for you if none of the aforementioned processes are a fit or if you want to complement one or more of the other processes. But what may influence whether it is appropriate for you is who the potential coaches are. The case study interview data suggested that this process is best used where the coach has significant and unique expertise to help the coachee to achieve personal and business goals. If this is not the case, then this process may not be suitable.

Knowing when you are using it

You are likely to be using this process if experiential learning, action learning and coaching principles, processes and practices resemble what occurs at your organisation to realise strategy. You may be a strategic leader with an informal coach that you go to and use as a sounding board and to receive constructive feedback and insights on intended strategic actions and past strategic actions. Alternatively, you could be a business owner, board chair or key shareholder using the coaching process to induct a new strategic leader or to optimise the performance of an existing strategic leader. The coaching relationship need not necessarily be formal; as with the best leaders, the coaching actions of some of the best coaches may not even be observable.

Process strengths and shortcomings

We identified three key strengths of this process. The first is its use of experiential learning, action learning and coaching practices to develop strategic leadership skills and to optimise the current and future performance of strategic leaders. Given the benefits of these practices, it is a great strength of this process to incorporate them into strategy execution. Second, the process enables realisation of both deliberate and emergent strategy. In the initial stages, it is largely focused on deliberate strategy, but as strategic leaders learn more from their experience and become more capable, then the balance shifts more towards realisation of emergent strategy. Finally, the Performance Monitoring and Coaching Process enables tapping into existing high potential employees and developing them into top strategic leaders. For some of the other strategy execution processes, strategic leadership know-how is assumed knowledge, and this may result in strategic leaders being brought in from outside of the organisation who already have the know-how at the senior level.

Common tips and traps

If you are using this process, we suggest you get a good understanding of the aims, benefits and effective practice of experiential learning, action learning and coaching processes. With such an understanding, you will be in a much better position to apply the Performance Monitoring and Coaching Process – which is heavily reliant on the aforementioned processes. We also suggest that you take care not to overreact negatively when strategic action implementations go wrong, as this may impede or even disable the experiential learning process.[16] Finally, we suggest that you remain vigilant to what the appropriate degree of constraint on the actions of coachees ought to be and how your corresponding coaching style needs to change to accommodate this, as coachees learn from their actions and improve their execution capabilities.

Spotlight on the role of strategic leaders

Like many other processes, the Performance Monitoring and Coaching Process requires hands-on strategic leadership involvement for strategic leaders to discharge their important responsibility of ensuring the realisation of strategies that achieve the optimal balance between efficiency and adaptation. Specifically, this process requires that coaches or strategic leadership overseers have an intimate understanding of the internal and external environment to enable formation of the right strategies. Coaches then need to have a strong understanding of experiential learning, action learning and coaching process and practice to be able to apply these practices to optimise strategic leaders' learning and performance. Until a new strategic leader builds their strategy execution capability and confidence, their overseer or coach remains largely accountable for strategy execution.

What if you are not a strategic leader?

If you are not a strategic leader, one of the best ways to influence strategy is to consistently over-deliver on the roles and projects delegated to you by your leaders. In doing this, you will likely be promoted into roles with more responsibility and greater execution challenges. As you get promoted, you are likely to catch the attention of more senior strategic leaders. Once you have caught their attention, you can seek advice from them on what else you can do to better support realisation of the organisation's strategies. For example, you can ask for more and more challenging projects to use to build your strategy execution capabilities. Over time, such leaders may seek you out for challenging projects, and as you continue to over-deliver on such projects, a strategic leader may seek you out for a strategic leadership role which you may not be yet ready for, but can grow into with the right support. You may then have the opportunity to learn strategic leadership through experiential learning and coaching.

Notes

1 Busulwa, R. (2017). *The relationship between strategy execution and complexity* (Ph.D. Thesis). University of South Australia, Adelaide, SA.
2 Kolb, D. A. (2014). *Experiential learning: Experience as the source of learning and development.* Upper Saddle River, NJ: FT press.
3 Senge, P. (1990). *The fifth discipline. The art & practice of the learning organization.* New York, NY: Doubleday Currency.
4 Irwin, T. (2000). *Nicomachean ethics.* Indianapolis, IN: Hackett Publishing.
5 Moon, J. A. (2013). *A handbook of reflective and experiential learning: Theory and practice.* London, England: Routledge.
6 Kolb, D. (1984). *Experiential learning: Experience as the source of learning and development* (p. 21). Englewood Cliffs, NJ: Prentice Hall.
7 Kraft, R. G. (1994). Bike riding and the art of learning. In L. B. Barnes, C. Roland Christensen, & A. J. Hansen (Eds.), *Teaching and the case method.* Boston, MA: Harvard Business School Press.
8 Senge, P. (1990). *The fifth discipline. The art & practice of learning organization.* New York, NY: Doubleday Currency.
9 Cox, E., Bachkirova, T., & Clutterbuck, D. A. (Eds.). (2014). *The complete handbook of coaching.* London, England: Sage.
10 Stober, D. R., & Grant, A. M. (Eds.). (2010). *Evidence based coaching handbook: Putting best practices to work for your clients.* Hoboken, NJ: John Wiley & Sons.
11 Cox, E., Bachkirova, T., & Clutterbuck, D. A. (Eds.). (2014). *The complete handbook of coaching.* London, England: Sage.

12 Stober, D. R., & Grant, A. M. (Eds.). (2010). *Evidence based coaching handbook: Putting best practices to work for your clients.* Hoboken, NJ: John Wiley & Sons.
13 Hersey, P., & Blanchard, K. H. (1969). "Life cycle theory of leadership". *Training and Development Journal, 23*(5), 26–34.
14 Hersey, P. (1985). *The situational leader.* New York, NY: Warner Books.
15 Bennis, W. (2004). The seven ages of a leader, *Harvard Business Review,* January.
16 Coutu, D. (2006). Ideas as an art. *Harvard Business Review,* October.

13 The Project Management Process

Origin and design principles

Origin

Project management as a discipline has been around since the 1950s[1] and is concerned with initiating, planning, executing, controlling and closing (or finishing) the work of a team to deliver on specific goals or outcomes within required constraints (e.g. within time, quality, budget and other constraints).[2] This is usually in a context of a changing internal and external business environment that continually threatens the achievement of goals and outcomes and the adherence to required constraints.[3] It is for this reason that delivering project outcomes on time, to quality and within budget and other constraints is accepted to be a real challenge for most organisations.[4] As applied to strategy execution, project management usually involves using one or more Project Management Processes to deliver projects, which in turn contribute to the realisation of strategic objectives or strategic initiatives.[5,6] Project management can be used to realise deliberate strategy by translating strategic objectives into specific projects or groups of projects and then using one or more Project Management Processes to deliver those projects.[7] Delivery of the projects results in realisation of strategic objectives, assuming that the strategic objectives were translated into the correct projects. Project management can also be used to realise emergent strategy, as employees can form their own autonomous initiatives and use one or more Project Management Processes to realise these initiatives. To the extent that these initiatives are delivered and end up enhancing the organisation's longevity, then they contribute to the realisation of emergent strategy. In our case study interviews and surveys, we found six Project Management Processes or methodologies being used to execute strategic initiatives.

The problem

Strategic leaders often face challenges effectively communicating strategy and aligning the actions of employees to efficiently and effectively execute strategy. In addition, many strategy execution processes require the people leading strategy execution to have sufficient strategy execution know-how and access to strategy execution tools. This know-how usually consists of a body of knowledge and experience. Even where strategic leaders resolve the communication, alignment, know-how and execution tools challenges, critical parts of the organisation need to understand the approach to strategy execution and accept it as fitting with their logic about how execution should work.[8,9] Project Management Processes offer a solution to many of these challenges. For starters, a certain level of strategy alignment is implicit in Project Management Processes when projects are derived from strategic objectives. Second, most Project Management Processes have inbuilt communication and authorisation activities that can be used to deliver targeted communication regarding the purpose and value of the project to the organisation. Finally, project management approaches and processes are generally well known and accepted ways of working that fit with the institutional logic of most organisations. Because of this, people in all parts of the organisation are likely to understand what the strategy is and what may be required of them once the strategy is translated into specific projects. There is also a readily available industry of project management professionals, a clear and abundant body of knowledge on project management and an abundance of tools that can be used to facilitate project processes.

The idea in brief

The key steps in using project management to realise strategy are as follows: (1) develop clear strategic objectives, (2) translate strategic objectives into specific projects that will achieve these objectives, (3) use appropriate Project Management Processes to deliver projects, and (4) learn from intended and unintended results to improve future efforts. In what follows, we unpack each step and, for Step 3, we provide a brief overview of each project management approach and the environments it was most used and effective in. Following this, we discuss the use of project management for strategy execution in general. That is, what we discuss can be taken to apply to each project management approach. We have not gone into much detail with each approach, as there is ample literature on each specific Project Management Process. We have also not provided a case study, as there are many readily available case studies in print on each Project Management Process (see Figure 13.1).

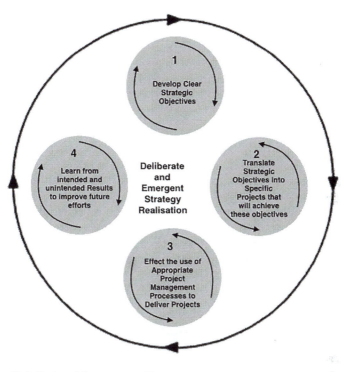

Figure 13.1 Project Management Processes.

Step 1: Develop clear strategic objectives – Similar to other strategy execution processes, the first step of this process is to develop the strategy. This will usually require top managers to do the ongoing groundwork of understanding changes in their internal and external environment, the implications of these changes for their organisation and the resultant immediate, medium and long-term opportunities and threats for their organisation. Armed with this understanding, they can then fulfil the requirements of Step 1 by identifying the priority strategic objectives for their organisation's immediate, medium and long-term future. These strategic objectives need to be specific, measurable, achievable, relevant and time-bound (SMART).

Step 2: Translate strategic objectives into specific projects that will achieve these objectives – In this step, strategic leaders devise specific projects which, if delivered, will result in achievement of the strategic objectives identified in step 1. One approach to this is to use

Strategy Maps to visually represent the strategy and outline the causal linkages between strategic objectives.[10] Then, measures of success for each strategic objective can be determined and used to set the targets to be achieved in order to realise each strategic objective. Projects or initiatives for the achievement of particular targets can then be devised.[11,12] As a part of this step, it is important that the projects formed have SMART deliverables or outcomes and that sufficient resources to deliver the projects are allocated.

Step 3: Effect the use of appropriate Project Management Processes to deliver projects – Having translated strategic objectives into specific projects, strategic leaders then need to ensure that they effect the use of Project Management Processes to deliver these projects and realise desired project outcomes. Depending on the organisation and the strategic leaders, this may be effected in a number of ways. In some organisations, it may involve acquiring specific project management expertise and delegating the delivery of projects to specialist project managers. This may require strategic leaders to select an appropriate Project Management Process for their context (e.g. Lean Project Management) and then hire project managers who are specialists in the use of that process. Other organisations may establish or use a project management office (PMO) and delegate the management and delivery of all projects to the PMO. In this case, the PMO may select the appropriate Project Management Processes to use in the delivery of each project. Here we provide a high-level view of the most common Project Management Processes we found in use to realise strategy.

Project Management Body of Knowledge (PMBOK)

The Project Management Body of Knowledge (PMBOK) process or methodology is made up of the following five process groups: initiating, planning, executing, monitoring/controlling and closing. These 5 process groups, in turn, unpack into 47 processes and are supported by the following knowledge areas: Project Integration Management, Project Scope Management, Project Time Management, Project Cost Management, Project Quality Management, Project Human Resource Management, Project Communications Management, Project Risk Management, Project Procurement Management and Project Stakeholders Management. We found this process to be used at large organisations in obvious, complicated and complex but low volatility environments but with projects that were large and had long delivery time frames.

Projects in Controlled Environments (PRINCE2)

The Projects in Controlled Environments Process or methodology emphasises dividing projects into manageable and controllable stages. It is made up of the following process groups: starting a project, initiating a project, directing a project, controlling a stage, managing product delivery, managing stage boundaries and closing a project. These process groups are supported by seven themes (Business Case, Organisation, Quality, Plans, Risk, Change and Progress). The process groups are also supported by seven principles (continued business justification, learning from experience, defined roles and responsibilities, management by stages, management by exception, focus on products and tailoring to suit the project environment). We also found this process to be mostly used at large organisations in obvious, complicated and complex but low volatility environments but with projects that were large and had long delivery time frames.

Lean Project Management

The Lean Project Management Process or approach focuses on the adoption of lean thinking principles and tools into the project management context. It emphasises delivering more value with less waste using lean principles and tools. Examples of Lean tools include 5S, Andon, Bottleneck Analysis, Continuous Flow, Gemba, Hoshin Kanri, Continuous Improvement, Just in Time, Error Proofing, PDCA and many more. The application of this process/methodology to strategy execution requires setting strategic objectives, translating these objectives into a strategic initiatives portfolio or group of projects and following the methodology to manage delivery of each initiative or project. We found this process to be in use in large organisations as well as small business and equally used across different environments.

Agile Project Management

This Project Management Process or approach focuses on continuous improvement, project scope flexibility, team input and delivering essential quality products. It consists of the following steps/stages: (1) identifying the product/service/outcome vision, (2) creating a product/service/outcome roadmap, (3) creating a product/service/outcome release plan, (4) undertaking sprint planning, (5) holding regular stand-up meetings, (6) undertaking sprint reviews and (7) holding sprint retrospectives. Agile Project Management adheres to the agile manifesto and agile project management principles, roles, artefacts and events. While Agile Project Management is more often used for product delivery in software development, applying it to strategy means replacing the term "product" with the term "strategic initiative or outcome", in the earlier mentioned steps. This project management approach was mostly cited in small businesses and in the private sector. It was half as common in large organisations. It was cited to the same degree across obvious, complicated, complex and chaotic environments.

Extreme Project Management

The Extreme Project Management Process or approach is usually used for managing chaotic, messy and unpredictable projects which require speed, innovation and just-in-time planning. It consists of the following steps: (1) creating a project plan which anticipates that everything may change, (2) answering the essential questions about the plan (who needs it and why, what will it take to do it, can the team get what it needs to finish it, is it worth it), (3) scheduling work in short cycles of a few weeks at max, (4) having a project kickoff meeting to give everyone a full rundown of everything involved and resolving any queries, (5) communicating with the project sponsor/client frequently and providing their feedback to the team, (6) following up work cycles with frequent check-in sessions and realignment meetings, and (7) celebrating every win as cycles finish. We found this process used across all organisational sizes and across all environments to about the same degree.

Step 4: Learn from intended and unintended results to improve future efforts – In this step, strategic leaders remain vigilant at all times to what is working well and what isn't working well so they can iteratively improve how they undertake activities within this process and/ or identify complementary process to run in parallel with this process.

Caveats

The steps or activities in this process are iterative, rather than being episodic and sequential. They're always at work, even if aspects of some may have to start before others. As with other processes, the activities of this process are the daily responsibility of strategic leaders.

Prevalence

We found 70 per cent of organisations, or nearly four in every five organisations, to be using Project Management Processes to some degree to execute strategy, although not necessarily using them in isolation. Usage of Project Management Processes was most common in the private sector, although NGO/NFP organisations and Government organisations weren't far behind, at 66 per cent and 53 per cent, respectively. Large and medium-sized organisations were greater users of project management processes (approximately 85% of such organisations) than small businesses (63% of such organisations). Usage was about the same across obvious, complicated, complex and chaotic environments. But Project Management Processes were most effective in obvious and complicated environments. Their effectiveness at executing strategy was more often associated with low to very low strategy execution effectiveness in complex, high volatility and chaotic environments (see Figure 13.2).

Are you in the right environment for this process?

Although Project Management Processes were used in all environments, we found them to be most effective in obvious, complicated and complex but low volatility environments. Thus, if you are in such an environment, then Project Management Processes may be ideal for achieving strategic objectives; but we found Project Management Processes to be less effective in complex but high volatility and chaotic environments. However, we noticed that less structured Project Management Processes (e.g. Agile, Extreme) were effective in such environments. Thus, if you are in such environments, then you may be in

Process	Sector				Employees (Org Size)				
	Public Sector / Government	Private Sector	NGO/NFP	All Sectors	>500	51-499	2 - 50	<2	All Sizes
7 Factor Process	10%	13%	25%	13%	19%	10%	10%	0%	12%
Execution Premium Process	24%	16%	25%	18%	25%	21%	13%	11%	18%
Simple Rules	14%	20%	17%	18%	13%	21%	23%	44%	21%
Lean Strategy Deployment Process	14%	19%	25%	18%	22%	21%	15%	11%	18%
Change Acceleration Process	14%	11%	17%	12%	9%	21%	10%	11%	12%
Project Management Process	53%	80%	66%	70%	88%	84%	63%	33%	72%
Talent Placement Process	14%	27%	25%	23%	22%	26%	23%	11%	22%
Outcomes and Incentives / Disincentives Communication Process	24%	28%	25%	26%	31%	26%	25%	11%	26%
Learning on the Run Process	39%	38%	50%	38%	31%	42%	43%	22%	37%
Resource Allocation / Portfolio Management Process	19%	17%	25%	18%	22%	21%	18%	66%	24%
Performance Monitoring and Feedback Process	39%	38%	50%	38%	44%	37%	43%	0%	38%

Figure 13.2 Proportion of study participants using a Project Management Process by sector or organisation size.*

Note: *For example, of the 241 study participants, 50 participants were from the public sector/government. Of these 50 public sector/government participants, 5 participants (10%) used the 7 Factor Process. This table differs from Tables 6.23 and 6.24 shown in Busulwa (2016), where process users in each sector are shown as a proportion of all study participants. So, in the case of public sector/government users of the 7 Factor Process, this is shown as 2% (i.e. 5/241 = 2%).

the right environment to use Project Management Processes, so long as you use low structure Project Management Processes. That is, if you are in a high velocity or chaotic environment, then a low structure Project Management Process, such as Extreme Project Management or Agile Project Management, is more likely to work than a high structure one, such as PMBOK. Finally, we observed that more structured Project Management Processes were more effective in large organisations, whereas low structured processes could be effective in both large and small organisations.

Knowing when you are using it

If delivering work through projects or any of the Project Management Processes discussed earlier are common at your organisation, you may be using this process to realise strategy. You may not be at the level where you see strategic objectives get formed and translated into projects, but you may hear of major projects being brought up in discussions of strategic achievements. At some organisations, this process may operate in parallel with other processes. For example, project management may be used for deliberate strategies that require project management's structure and discipline while more autonomous strategy processes are used to realise emergent strategy.

Process strengths and shortcomings

There are several strengths of using Project Management Process for strategy execution. First, project management is a long-established discipline for delivering project outcomes in an efficient and effective manner. Perhaps in part because of this, the use of Project Management Processes or tools is not questioned in most organisations. Second, translating strategic objectives into projects and using Project Management Processes to deliver projects reduces two common strategy execution risks – lack of strategic alignment and insufficient strategy communication. Once strategic objectives are translated into projects, a certain level of strategic alignment and strategy communication is already implicit in the Project Management Process. That is, it becomes less likely that people will misunderstand what the projects are and their individual roles in projects – especially when these projects have SMART deliverables. As we discussed earlier, there is also a readily available industry of project management professionals, a clear and abundant body of knowledge on project management practices and an abundance of tools that can be used to facilitate project processes. The main shortcoming of using Project Management Processes is that some processes contain so much structure and prescription that significant expert resources are required to use them. Even where such resources are available, these processes can significantly constrain improvisation and thus limit capacity to adapt to changing environments. Many Project Management Processes are also well designed for realising deliberate strategy but may be difficult to use to encourage the emergence and realisation of emergent strategy.

Common tips and traps

We suggest that you take great care to ensure that SMART strategic objectives are set upfront. This will make it easier to translate the strategic objectives into relevant projects. We also suggest that great care be taken to understand the causal relationships between desired strategic objectives and proposed projects to ensure that delivery of the projects will result in realisation of strategic objectives. Given the diversity in Project Management Processes and the diversity in their effectiveness across organisation sizes and environments, using this approach requires that you choose a Project Management Process suited to you and your unique context. Finally, realistic estimation of project resources, costs and required time frames for delivery can be a significant challenge. When resources are limited, it can be tempting to under-allocate project resources, but this can result in project failure and subsequently failure to achieve the relevant strategic outcomes. Thus, we suggest that great care is taken and appropriate expertise is used to get this right.

Spotlight on the role of strategic leaders

Strategic leaders play a critical role in the use of Project Management Processes to realise strategy. For a start, it is the job of strategic leaders to ensure the right strategic objectives are formed and that these objectives are then translated into the right projects that will lead their achievement. Once this is done, it is strategic leadership's role to ensure that projects are not set up to fail. For example, they should ensure that projects outcomes are clear and that projects are resourced adequately and championed. Strategic leaders should also be involved in the selection of Project Management Processes to use at the organisation, since that choice may result in the encouragement or stifling of deliberate or emergent strategy. Beyond this, strategic leaders can do a number of things to supercharge projects across the organisation. They can build project teams' purpose by communicating the strategy, justifying the strategy and explaining how the different projects directly contribute to the strategy. They can spot those going above and beyond to make great project contributions and publicly reward and celebrate them. They can model the right attitudes and behaviours for the organisations' leaders to support efficient and effective project delivery. There is almost no limit to how proactive a role strategic leaders can play to ensure that the right projects are done and done efficiently and effectively so as to maximise the efficient pursuit of today's opportunities and adaptation to tomorrow's threats and opportunities.

What if you are not a strategic leader?

If you are not a strategic leader, one of the best ways you can contribute to the strategy is continuously build and strengthen your project management and project leadership knowledge, skills and experience. You can then use this knowledge, skills and experience to be an efficient and effective project team member. Early on, you can get involved in as many projects as you can, learn as much as you can and get to know as many people as you can. As time goes on, you can focus your efforts on over-delivering on the more challenging projects or on high profile projects to start to build a reputation as someone who works effectively with others and can be relied on to over-deliver. By consistently over-delivering, you may soon find yourself in project leadership and project management roles. Such roles are your opportunity to further over-deliver and over time become the go-to person for organisation critical strategic projects.

Notes

1 Kwak, Y. H. (2005). A brief history of project management. In Elias G. Carayannis et al. (Eds.), *The story of managing projects* (9th ed.). Westport, CT: Praeger.
2 Nokes, S., & Kelly, S. (2007). *The definitive guide to project management: The fast track to getting the job done on time and on budget.* London, England: Pearson Education.
3 Thomas, J., & Mengel, T. (2008). Preparing project managers to deal with complexity–Advanced project management education. *International Journal of Project Management, 26*(3), 304–315.
4 Cicmil, S., Cooke-Davies, T., Crawford, L., & Richardson, K. (2009). *Exploring the complexity of projects: Implications of complexity theory for project management practice.* Newtown Square, PA: Project Management Institute.
5 Loch, C., & Kavadias, S. (2011). Implementing strategy through projects. In Morris, P.W.G et al (Eds.) *The Oxford handbook of project management.* Oxford, London: Oxford University Press.

6 Milosevic, D., & Srivannaboon, S. (2006). A theoretical framework for aligning project management with business strategy: Drivers, changes and benefits of adopting project-based management. *Project Management Journal, 37*(3), 98–110.

7 Pellegrinelli, S., & Bowman, C. (1994). Implementing strategy through projects. *Long Range Planning, 27*(4), 125–132.

8 Thornton, P. H., Ocasio, W., & Lounsbury, M. (2012). *The institutional logics perspective: A new approach to culture, structure and process.* Oxford, England: Oxford University Press on Demand.

9 Thornton, P. H., & Duke, I. (2002). The rise of the corporation in a craft industry: Conflict and conformity in institutional logics. *Academy of Management Journal, 45*(1), 101–181.

10 Kaplan, R. S., & Norton, D. P. (1996). Using the balanced scorecard as a strategic management system. *Harvard Business Review, 74*(1), 75–85.

11 Kaplan, R. S., & Norton, D. P. (2008). *The execution premium: Linking strategy to operations for competitive advantage.* Boston, MA: Harvard Business School Publishing.

12 Kaplan, R. S., & Norton, D. P. (1996). Using the balanced scorecard as a strategic management system. *Harvard Business Review, 74*(1), 75–85.

14 The Lean Start-Up and Agile Innovation Processes

Origin and design principles

Origin

Lean Startup and Agile Innovation Processes apply Lean Thinking and/ or Agile Manifesto values, principles and tools to the process of introducing new products, services or solutions.[1,2] In doing so, proponents of these processes argue they accelerate the speed, minimise the risk and optimise the customer value of new product, service or solution introductions.[3,4] The application of Lean Thinking and Agile Methodology values, principles and tools first surfaced during our case study interviews as Lean Strategy Deployment and Agile Project Management processes. In the broader cross-section surveys, there was unexpected citing of Lean Startup and Agile Innovation Processes in the strategy execution context. Initially, we disagreed on whether these were in fact product development processes being confused for strategy execution processes. When we researched these processes further, we found ample examples of them indeed being used to realise strategic initiatives. In some instances, these strategic initiatives were products and services. In other instances, these were broad objectives and outcomes. In both cases, the same approach was used, albeit the customers may have changed from external buyers to internal stakeholders such as the Board, the CEO, the Executive Team or the Strategy Management Office.

The first of these processes, the Lean Startup, combines business-hypothesis-driven experimentation, iterative product releases and validated learning to shorten product/service or solution development cycles.[5] It proposes that a minimum viable version of the product/service or solution is built as fast as possible and put in the hands of the customer in order to start gathering customer feedback. This feedback is then used in subsequent iterations of the process or new product versions until a unique and valuable product/service/solution that fits with a valuable market or stakeholder is delivered.[6] The Lean Startup was introduced in 2008 and emerged from entrepreneur and investor Eric Ries' experiences applying Lean and Agile management principles to high technology start-up companies.

The second process, Agile Innovation, applies Agile values, principles and tools to the process and practice of innovation.[7,8,9] In this process, products/services or solutions are built incrementally through one to four-week work cycles (or sprints) by small, focused and self-governing teams. Sprints are planned so that each sprint results in the next most important element of the product/service/solution being delivered for review by the customer or stakeholder. The customer review is followed by a team review of the effectiveness of that sprint and of how the efficiency and effectiveness of future sprints can be maximised. Customer feedback and sprint retrospective information feeds back into revised sprint plans. Iterations of the process and of the product/service/solution occur faster and better until the product/service/solution delivers unique and important value to important customers or stakeholders.[10] Proponents of this process argue that it accelerates the speed of innovation, significantly decrease risk in the innovation effort and better engages innovating teams.[11]

The problem

Lean Startup and Agile Innovation Processes solve four critical problems. First, these processes offer a way to minimise the waste often associated with new product/service/solution introductions due to redundant activities and processes, low-value-add product and service features, misguided capital allocation and pursuit of the efficient provision of products/services/solutions that are no longer of value.[12,13,14,15] Identification and elimination of waste is an important building block of Lean Thinking and Lean Thinking is an important antecedent to Agile.[16] Second, Lean Startup and Agile Innovation Processes provide a way for organisations to incrementally and iteratively explore, validate and adapt their solutions to opaque market or stakeholder needs in collaboration with those customers or stakeholders.[17,18,19,20] Using this approach, organisations can incrementally step up their resource commitments to product/service/solution ideas. This removes the risks of large initial capital outlays, high profile initiative failures and bets based on predictions that are unlikely to work out.[21] Third, both processes provide near real-time flexibility to changes in customer/stakeholder needs and changes in the business environment with minimal cost.[22]

Finally, both processes have been argued to better engage teams to intro-
duce new products/services/solutions and to do this in the most efficient
and effective way.[23]

The idea in brief

As there are ample online resources on both of these processes, we have
not unpacked them in detail here. Instead, we outline some of the key
resources where you can find high-level overviews or more detailed
unpacking of the processes, case studies of the processes in action and
common tips and traps. For a high-level overview of the Lean Startup
Process, we recommend Steve Blank's May 2013 Harvard Business
Review article, *How the Lean Startup Changes Everything*. For a more
detailed unpacking of the process, common tips and traps and a range
of case studies of the Lean Startup Process in action, we suggest Eric
Ries' seminal texts *The Lean Startup* and *The Startup Way*, as well as the
companion website, with a range of resources in different formats. For
a high-level overview of the Agile Innovation Process, we recommend
Bain and Company's 2016 *Executive Guide to Agile Innovation*. We also
recommend the May 2016 Harvard Business Review article, *Embracing
Agile*. This article was written by Darrell Rigby, head of global innovation practice at Bain and Company; Jeff Sutherland, CEO of Scrum
Inc. and co-creator of the scrum form of Agile; and Hirotaka Takeuchi,
professor of strategy at Harvard Business School. For a more detailed
unpacking of the Agile Innovation Process, common tips and traps and
related case studies of the process in action, we suggest Langdon Morris,
Moses Ma and Po Chi Wu's book *Agile Innovation: the revolutionary approach to accelerate success, inspire engagement, and ignite creativity*.

Similar to the use of project management processes to realise strategy, we suggest that use of these processes be complemented with the
ongoing work of understanding changes in the internal and external
environment, the implications of these changes for the organisation
and the resultant immediate, medium and long-term opportunities and
threats for the organisation. This will enable strategic leaders to form
the right strategic objectives that can then be pursued with either the
Lean Startup or Agile Innovation Process.

What you might know it as

We weren't able to test the prevalence and effectiveness of Lean Startup and
Agile Innovation Processes in different environments, as they came onto
our radar in the free-form feedback fields of the final survey questionnaire.

However, researchers and practitioners suggest that these processes are most effective in settings similar to those of software innovation.[24] That is, settings that require solutions to complex problems where the solution cannot be known in advance, where customer requirements are likely to change part way through the implementation, where the work can be compartmentalised and where the delivery of such work requires self-managing teams working in collaboration with customers or stakeholders.[25] It is also worth carefully considering the risks of these processes in some contexts.

Are you in the right environment for this process?

We also didn't have the opportunity to test the prevalence and effectiveness of Lean Startup and Agile Innovation Processes in different environments. But, as we noted earlier, research suggests that these processes are most effective in environments that require solutions to complex problems where the solution cannot be known in advance, where customer requirements are likely to change part way through, where the work can be compartmentalised and where the delivery of such work requires self-managing teams working in collaboration with customers or stakeholders.[26]

Knowing when you are using it

You are likely to be using the Lean Startup Process if the steps described earlier fit with your organization's approach to new product introductions or to the pursuit of strategic initiatives. Other telltale signs include the use concepts such as "build, measure, learn", "Minimum Viable Product", "Pivoting", "Business Model Canvas", "Continuous Delivery", "Actionable Metrics" and "Innovation Accounting".[27] This terminology is unique to the Lean Startup Process and differs from other Lean Thinking applications to strategy execution such as Hoshin Planning and Lean Project Management. You are likely to be using the Agile Innovation Process if the Agile Innovation activities we described earlier resemble your organisation's approach to innovation. Other telltale signs include the regular use of the terms "Sprint Planning", "Sprints", "Sprint Retrospectives" or "Sprint Reviews", "Customer Review" or "Initiative Owner Review", "Agile Principles" and "Agile Values". As with earlier strategy execution processes, it is possible you may use this process in parallel with other processes. For example, your organisation may be using this process to realise a product innovation strategy while using different processes in parallel to realise other types of strategies.

Process strengths and shortcomings

Key strengths of these processes lie in their ability to provide a simple way to identify and minimise waste,[28] to be flexible to changing customer/stakeholder needs and changes in the business environment,[29] to incrementally and iteratively explore, validate and adapt new solutions to opaque markets or stakeholder needs in collaboration with those customers or stakeholders[30] and to engage small teams to apply Agile in the most efficient and effective way.[31]

Spotlight on the role of strategic leaders

Strategic leaders can supercharge the effectiveness of these processes for strategy realisation by first getting a true understanding of them and how they work best. Having done this, strategic leaders then need to consider the best ways to engage, motivate and provide impetus to Agile leaders and teams to operate at optimal efficiency and effectiveness. One powerful way they can do this is to apply the processes themselves. For example, the CEO may bring the executive team together to operate as an Agile team. In doing so, they will come to understand the experiences, behaviours and challenges that may be encountered by other Agile teams. With this experiential understanding, they will be in a position to speak the language of Agile teams, to know the key pain points of these teams and the critical points at which to intervene to optimise engagement, confidence, speed and effectiveness. In turn, the board chair may bring together the board as an Agile team and be in a position to better engage with the CEO and executive team's efforts.

What if you are not a strategic leader?

If you are not a strategic leader, there are several ways you can optimise your contribution to the organisation's strategy through these processes. We first recommend that you get a good understanding of the Lean Startup and Agile Innovation Processes.[32] For example, you could set a time frame to make yourself a subject matter expert in these processes. This will likely give you a good understanding of the values, principles, practices and tools underpinning these processes. We also suggest you develop your strategic thinking skills so that you can start to understand what the organisation's strategy is, why strategic leaders have chosen that strategy, their approach to executing the strategy and the effectiveness of the strategy and the execution of that strategy. Being able to think this way may enable you to spot product/service/solution opportunities that have not previously been considered. Second, we suggest that you look for opportunities to be involved in Agile teams and that you incrementally build your ability to be a high contributing Agile team member through contributions on successive sprints and Agile teams. We then suggest that you seek out opportunities to join high-functioning Agile teams and ones working on challenging and mission critical projects. You are likely to learn valuable insights into what it takes for an Agile team to succeed. You can then seek out opportunities to learn how to lead Agile teams.

Notes

1 Rigby, D. K., Sutherland, J., & Takeuchi, H. (2016). The secret history of agile innovation. *Harvard Business Review*, April.
2 Ries, E. (2011). *The lean startup: How today's entrepreneurs use continuous innovation to create radically successful businesses.* New York, NY: Crown Books.
3 Morris, L., Ma, M., & Wu, P. C. (2014). *Agile innovation: The revolutionary approach to accelerate success, inspire engagement, and ignite creativity.* Hoboken, NJ: John Wiley & Sons.
4 Ries, E. (2011). *The lean startup: How today's entrepreneurs use continuous innovation to create radically successful businesses.* Crown Books.
5 Morris, L., Ma, M., & Wu, P. C. (2014). *Agile innovation: The revolutionary approach to accelerate success, inspire engagement, and ignite creativity.* Hoboken, NJ: John Wiley & Sons.
6 Blank, S. (2013). Why the lean start-up changes everything. *Harvard Business Review, 91*(5), 63–72.
7 Rigby, D. K., Sutherland, J., & Takeuchi, H. (2016). The secret history of agile innovation. *Harvard Business Review*, April.
8 Rigby, D. K., Sutherland, J., & Takeuchi, H. (2016). Embracing agile. *Harvard Business Review, 94*(5), 40–50.
9 Morris, L., Ma, M., & Wu, P. C. (2014). *Agile innovation: The revolutionary approach to accelerate success, inspire engagement, and ignite creativity.* Hoboken, NJ: John Wiley & Sons.
10 Rigby, D. K., Sutherland, J., & Takeuchi, H. (2016). Embracing agile. *Harvard Business Review, 94*(5), 40–50.
11 Morris, L., Ma, M., & Wu, P. C. (2014). *Agile innovation: The revolutionary approach to accelerate success, inspire engagement, and ignite creativity.* Hoboken, NJ: John Wiley & Sons.
12 Rigby, D. K., Sutherland, J., & Takeuchi, H. (2016). The secret history of agile innovation. *Harvard Business Review*, April.
13 Rigby, D. K., Sutherland, J., & Takeuchi, H. (2016). Embracing agile. *Harvard Business Review, 94*(5), 40–50.
14 Morris, L., Ma, M., & Wu, P. C. (2014). *Agile innovation: The revolutionary approach to accelerate success, inspire engagement, and ignite creativity.* Hoboken, NJ: John Wiley & Sons.
15 Ries, E. (2011). *The lean startup: How today's entrepreneurs use continuous innovation to create radically successful businesses.* Crown Books.
16 Putnik, G. D., & Putnik, Z. (2012). Lean vs agile in the context of complexity management in organizations. *The Learning Organization, 19*(3), 248–266.

17 Rigby, D. K., Sutherland, J., & Takeuchi, H. (2016). The secret history of agile innovation. *Harvard Business Review,* April.
18 Rigby, D. K., Sutherland, J., & Takeuchi, H. (2016). Embracing agile. *Harvard Business Review, 94*(5), 40–50.
19 Morris, L., Ma, M., & Wu, P. C. (2014). *Agile innovation: The revolutionary approach to accelerate success, inspire engagement, and ignite creativity.* Hoboken, NJ: John Wiley & Sons.
20 Ries, E. (2011). *The lean startup: How today's entrepreneurs use continuous innovation to create radically successful businesses.* Crown Books.
21 Ries, E. (2011). *The lean startup: How today's entrepreneurs use continuous innovation to create radically successful businesses.* Crown Books.
22 Rigby, D. K., Sutherland, J., & Takeuchi, H. (2016). Embracing agile. *Harvard Business Review, 94*(5), 40–50.
23 Rigby, D. K., Sutherland, J., & Takeuchi, H. (2016). Embracing agile. *Harvard Business Review, 94*(5), 40–50.
24 Rigby, D. K., Sutherland, J., & Takeuchi, H. (2016). Embracing agile. *Harvard Business Review, 94*(5), 40–50.
25 Rigby, D. K., Sutherland, J., & Takeuchi, H. (2016). Embracing agile. *Harvard Business Review, 94*(5), 40–50.
26 Rigby, D. K., Sutherland, J., & Takeuchi, H. (2016). Embracing agile. *Harvard Business Review, 94*(5), 40–50.
27 Ries, E. (2011). *The lean startup: How today's entrepreneurs use continuous innovation to create radically successful businesses.* Crown Books.
28 Rigby, D. K., Sutherland, J., & Takeuchi, H. (2016). Embracing agile. *Harvard Business Review, 94*(5), 40–50.
29 Rigby, D. K., Sutherland, J., & Takeuchi, H. (2016). Embracing agile. *Harvard Business Review, 94*(5), 40–50.
30 Blank, S. (2013). Why the lean start-up changes everything. *Harvard Business Review, 91*(5), 63–72.
31 Rigby, D. K., Sutherland, J., & Takeuchi, H. (2016). The secret history of agile innovation. *Harvard Business Review,* April.
32 Rigby, D. K., Sutherland, J., & Takeuchi, H. (2016). Embracing agile. *Harvard Business Review, 94*(5), 40–50.

Part III

Thriving in complex environments

15 Thriving in complex environments

The role of alert strategic leaders

Expect more and more surprising events and disruptions

Increasing complexity and volatility inevitably leads to a corresponding increase in the number of unexpected events facing the firm and often significant, even fatal, disruption.[1,2] As we have discussed earlier, surprising events and disruptions often require abandoning existing strategic initiatives in order to adapt to threats posed. This can result in significant economic, brand, customer and employee engagement damage if not properly managed. In some cases, disruption can threaten the very survival of a firm. Thus, strategic leaders are faced with an important challenge: How to adapt to unexpected events and how to do this whilst minimising risk?

Challenges of adapting to surprising events and disruptions

Stanford Professor of Management Robert Burgelman's study into organisational approaches to adapting to changed environments identified four common approaches to adaptation.[3] In the first approach, which we refer to as "The Status Quo", organisations succumb to the pressures of path dependence[4] and do what they've always done, in spite of seemingly obvious environmental changes or public strategic statements they may make to the contrary. In the second approach, which we refer to as "Incremental Adjustments", organisations make incremental changes to peripheral features of the strategy but leave much of the overall core strategy unchanged. Robert Burgelman found that the first two approaches often result in changes in the external environment outpacing organisation changes and eventually overwhelming it.[5] Organisations using these two approaches eventually find themselves in crisis survival situations not so different to those Louis Gerstner found at IBM[6] and Meg Whitman found at Hewlett Packard.[7] In both situations, external environment changes outpaced internal changes over a period of time until the organisations found themselves in a serious fight for market relevance and continued existence. Facing such situations, organisations usually turn to the third approach, "Reorientation". In this approach, strategic leaders make extreme and vacillating changes in the strategy that involve risky bets in order to remain viable.[8] Organisations fortunate enough to make it through such change crises to remain viable often lose much of their lustre in the process, and those not able to find a new footing often accelerate their demise. Burgelman found that although "Status Quo" and "Incremental Adjustments" type approaches risk having an organisation's strategy being overwhelmed by changes in complexity over time, reorientation was hardly the answer, since it involves make or break bets and significant disruption to existing strategy processes.[9] On this basis, he proposed a fourth approach: "Strategic Renewal". In this approach, organisations undertake ongoing exploration and experimentation to discover and test future adaptation opportunities well before the organisation's survival depends on them. Such exploration and experimentation can range from but isn't limited to internal corporate venturing, autonomous strategic initiatives, war games, scenario planning and acquisition of promising start-ups. Firms like Intel have used this approach for decades to remain key players in the high-velocity information technology industry, even in the face of constant and rapid obsolescence in core products.[10]

Why ambidexterity is the answer

In the real world, strategic leaders face dual and contradictory pressures to be efficient in the management of today's business while also ensuring they are able to adapt to tomorrow's opportunities and threats.[11] Ambidexterity, the ability to exploit today's opportunities and meet short-term performance expectations while at the same time exploring and preparing for future opportunities, is the answer to this contradiction.[12,13] Strategic leaders intuitively understand that they need to exploit short-term opportunities to remain relevant and solvent in short term and to fund the exploration and experimentation necessary to discover and exploit future opportunities. Essentially, thriving in complex environments depends on how well ambidexterity is put into effect and sustained as an enduring capability.[14,15] In the same way that an ambidextrous basketball player, one proficient in the use of both their left and right hands, is a more formidable offensive and defensive threat, an ambidextrous organisation is more of a competitive threat, especially in dynamic environments.

Different approaches to ambidexterity

The current body of ambidexterity research has identified a range of different levers for enabling ambidexterity as well as approaches to using these levers.[16] Strategic leaders can change levers such as the organisation structure, strategy execution processes, the employee context or their leadership style.[17] We discuss each lever in more detail, with the exception of ambidextrous leadership styles, for which there is abundant literature available.

Structural levers

Changing structural levers involves changing the organisation's structure in such a way as to have separate organisational units (i.e. business units, functions or companies) that pursue exploitation of current opportunities and those that explore and capture future opportunities. This approach often requires discrete business models. An organisation might, for example, operate its primary business as one business unit and its innovation and commercialisation business as another business unit. This way, it can cultivate appropriate control, operational discipline and efficiency in the first business unit and cultivate autonomy, flexibility and creativity in the second business unit. For example, consider Google's formation of Alphabet Inc., Google Ventures and Google Inc. business units to pursue both exploration and exploitation.

Process levers

Changing process levers involves changing strategy execution processes to have execution processes that enable realisation of exploratory strategies (or emergent strategies) and execution processes that enable realisation of exploitation strategies (or deliberate strategies). Emergent strategy processes are usually low in structure or level of constraint on the actions of employees and teams. This frees employees and teams to improvise, to adapt to change and to form autonomous strategic initiatives. Deliberate strategy processes are usually high in structure; that is, they limit the autonomous and improvisatory actions of employees to enable them to efficiently carry out prescribed activities. For example, Intel operates both deliberate and emergent strategy processes, referring to them as "induced" and "autonomous" strategy processes. Over many decades, the emergent or exploratory strategy process has enabled Intel to discover emerging technology opportunities prior to the decline of existing core products. And the deliberate or exploitation strategy process has enabled the organisation to maximise the value generated from established cash cows. For example, in 2003, as Intel's core product started to show signs of decline, strategic leaders were delighted to find that a team within the emergent or "autonomous" strategy process had invented a processor for mobile technologies that showed significant promise. On understanding the potential of the new processor, senior management was quick to scale up its investment in the new processor. The processor was rebranded the "Centrino" processor and the company spent hundreds of millions of dollars to refine it, market it, distribute it and scale it so it could become the company's next key growth platform.

In our study, we found that highly structured processes (e.g. the Execution Premium and 7 Factor Processes) worked better in obvious, complicated and complex but low volatility environments, that is, environments ideal for deliberate or exploitation strategies. In contrast, we found that low structure processes (e.g. Simple Rules, Talent Scouting) worked better in complex but high volatility and chaotic environments, that is, environments requiring realisation of emergent strategies. Given the different strategy execution processes we have identified, strategic leaders can combine one or more high structure processes with one or more low structure processes to achieve an optimal level of ambidexterity. Leaders can then vary the degree each type of process is utilised and the resources invested in it. By doing this, they can shape an optimal balance between efficiency and adaptation. For example, at points when it needed to identify the next big product opportunity, Intel ramped up resources allocated to low structure strategy processes until the next big product opportunity emerged. Once that product opportunity had emerged, Intel shifted this product to the high structure strategy processes for exploitation. To maximise exploitation, Intel scaled back some of the resources allocated to the low structure strategy process and ramped up resources in the high structure strategy process. For example, in 1975, Intel allocated 75 per cent of its resources to the high structure process and 25 per cent to low structure processes to maximise exploitation. But in 2005, it had 50 per cent of its resources allocated to low structure processes and 50 per cent to the high structure process to maximise exploration (this may have been due to the company escalating its resource commitment to the new Centrino processor that had emerged in the autonomous process. Figure 15.1 shows which processes should be used as complexity changes and which types of strategies are realised more.

Employee context levers

Changing employee levers involves creating an environment that enables and encourages individuals to make their own judgements

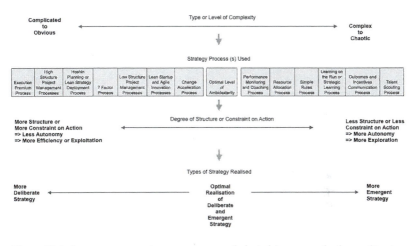

Figure 15.1 Strategy execution processes and their bias towards the realisation of deliberate and emergent strategies.

about how they pursue the competing demands for alignment and adaptability. A range of vehicles can be used to shift this lever, including culture, mission, vision, values, policies, leadership style and incentives and disincentives. For example, 3M used to enable and encourage its scientists and engineers to pursue alignment and adaptability by allowing them to spend 15 per cent of their time on exploratory and experimental projects of their choosing.[18] It also complemented this with freedom to form new venture teams and the ability to request seed capital.[19] These vehicles, along with other efforts at 3M, contribute to creating an environment where employees can make their own judgements about how to pursue the competing demands for alignment and adaptability.

Darwinian, sequential or simultaneous ambidexterity

In addition to using one or more of the levers we have just discussed, strategic leaders can take a Darwinian,[20] sequential or simultaneous approach to the levers. In the Darwinian approach, competing structures, processes and contexts face continuous environmental selection pressures and jostle for prominence until a winner emerges. The structures, processes and employee contexts that maximise efficiency and exploration are the ones that prevail and enjoy continued use. In the sequential approach, strategic leaders change the structure, process or context in use, depending on the environmental complexity faced at the

Levers ↓ Approaches ➤	Darwinian Natural Selection or Survival of the Fittest	Sequential or situational Exploration and Exploitation Over Time	Simultaneous Exploration and Exploitation
Organisation Structures	Example: Branded Venture Capital Organisation	Example: Temporal Commercialisation Units	Example: Permanent Corporate Venturing Unit operating in parallel with an organisation's normal operations
Strategy Execution Processes	Example: Leaders free to use whatever processes work but only leaders that get results get rewarded	Example: Use exploration processes to discover promising opportunities then cease these processes and use exploitation processes to exploit those opportunities	Example: use both exploration and exploitation processes at the same time
Employee Context	Example: Let the environment dictate employee impetus for exploration or exploitation actions	Example: Temporarily create conditions that encourage exploration until a promising new product is discovered - then cease exploration and go back to exploitation	Example: Institutionalise conditions that provide impetus for both exploration and exploitation actions
Leadership Style	E.g. Let the environment dictate which leadership styles achieve exploration or exploitation	Effect one type of leadership style at particular times and another type of leadership style at other times	Effect leadership styles that at all times encourage both exploration and exploitation activities

Figure 15.2 Combining forms of ambidexterity and approaches to those forms.

time. For example, an organisation using process-based ambidexterity may use the Execution Premium Process while facing a complicated environment to maximise its efficiency, but when the environmental context changes to chaotic, the organisation may switch to the Simple Rules Process to enable more improvisation and adaptive actions. That is, it sequentially changes between exploration to exploitation as the situation demands. This approach may become a challenge if the rate of change in complexity and type of complexity is fast and dynamic. Finally, in the simultaneous ambidexterity approach, exploration and exploitation are pursued in parallel. For example, an organisation may have in place both exploration and exploitation enabling structures, processes and or contexts. In Figure 15.2 we provide a matrix with an example of a way each lever and approach can be combined, notwithstanding that there are almost an unlimited number of ways the levers and approaches could be combined.

Role of alert strategic leadership

As discussed earlier, strategic leaders are the people on the top management team or the dominant coalition within the organisation. Their most important role is to ensure the realisation of strategies that balance the efficient pursuit of today's opportunities with building capacity to adapt to tomorrow's opportunities and threats. In more complex environments, this role becomes more pronounced. To thrive in such complex environments, our study suggests that strategic leaders should focus on four key areas: (1) effecting an appropriate form of ambidexterity, (2) maintaining an optimal balance between exploration and exploitation efforts, (3) fighting the negative effects of complexity on employee and stakeholder engagement, and (4) performing the essential activities that catalyse strategy execution in complex environments.

Effect an appropriate form of ambidexterity

It is the responsibility of strategic leaders at the board and/or executive team level to institute one or more forms of ambidexterity at their organisation and to ensure that the instituted form enables reliable realisation of exploration and exploitation strategies. As we have discussed, this involves configuring structural, process and/or contextual ambidexterity levers to enable both exploration and exploitation activities. These can be configured for ambidexterity to occur simultaneously, sequentially or situationally (through natural selection or through manual modification). Effecting the right form of ambidexterity goes a long way towards enabling strategic leaders to ensure they realise the right strategies that will maintain the long-term viability of the organisation. Some processes will have a degree of ambidexterity built in and, if using dual processes is too challenging, an alternative approach may be to loosen or tighten constraints in particular steps or activities within the process to achieve the desired level of deliberate and emergent strategy realisation. For example, an organisation using the Simple Rules Process may make the rules very restrictive to encourage deliberate strategy realisation or it may loosen them to encourage more emergent strategy realisation.

Maintain an optimal balance between exploration and exploitation efforts[21,22,23]

Since organisations operate in a competitive context, it is not enough to be able to realise exploration and exploitations strategies. Organisations must also do this more efficiently and effectively than current and potential competitors. Thus, strategic leaders must ensure that the forms of ambidexterity they put into effect dynamically optimise the deliberate and emergent strategy realisation efforts to maximise overall value creation. Changing the balance of efforts may occur through the degree of resources allocated, the extent to which a particular type of strategy process is used or other means. This comes to life in the example of Intel ramping up resources allocated to exploitation processes once its exploration processes had uncovered a highly promising product. In contrast, when Intel needed to increase the number and potential of products coming out of the exploration process, it would ramp up resources allocated to that process relative to those allocated to the exploitation process.

Fight the negative effects of complexity on employee and stakeholder engagement[24]

As we discussed earlier, employees and stakeholders form assumptions about the cause and effect relationships behind events occurring inside and outside their organisation. They then derive meanings from these assumptions and make predictions about the future of their organisations. These meanings and predictions influence employees' motivation and engagement to execute strategy. But increases in complexity result in these assumptions, meanings and predictions becoming more and more incorrect. Strategic leaders need to be vigilant to the effects of these assumptions, meanings and predictions. Where the effects are negative, strategic leaders need to challenge and correct the assumptions, meanings and predictions. By doing this, they will shape logics, meanings and predictions that drive engagement and accelerate strategy execution effectiveness.

Focus on particular activities that supercharge strategy execution in complex environments[25]

Our research revealed that irrespective of the approach to strategy execution taken, the quality and speed with which particular strategy execution activities were performed had an outsized positive effect on strategy execution effectiveness. These particular activities included strategy consultation, strategy communication, strategy justification, purpose building, engagement building, incentives and disincentives alignment and use of appropriate IT infrastructure to facilitate strategy execution activities. As used in our study, strategy consultation referred to genuine seeking and reflection of employees' input into the strategy, as opposed to the token efforts that often occur. Strategy communication referred to ensuring that everyone in the organisation understands what the strategy is. Most organisations do some form of strategy communication. The issue is the number of stakeholders reached, the quality of the message and the speed with which the message reaches them (needless to say, the approach to communication will differ across organisations). Strategy justification referred to convincing the organisation's stakeholders that the proposed strategy is actually the right strategy for the organisation. If stakeholders know the strategy but don't believe in it, they are more likely to engage in misaligned behaviours and activities. Purpose building is concerned with providing employees with the opportunity to make a meaningful contribution to a higher purpose beyond themselves. As it relates to strategy execution, it is concerned with identifying, communicating and justifying the higher purpose behind the strategy. Examples of organisations doing this well include Google, an organisation with the higher purpose mission "to organize the world's information, and make it universally accessible and useful", with every product and initiative intended to get it closer to achieving this mission. Purpose-driven organisations have been shown to outperform their peers in stock price by a factor of 12.[26] Engagement is concerned with ensuring employees buy into the strategy, understand the role they can play in the strategy and are motivated to play that role. If people are engaged, they're more likely to spend their time in strategically aligned activities rather than non-aligned activities. Aligning incentives and disincentives refers to ensuring that both incentives and disincentives encourage behaviours that support the strategy, rather than being at odds. Finally, the appropriate IT infrastructure activity is concerned with having the most effective software platform to support strategy execution. Such software platforms can improve strategy execution by easing communication, allocation of workflows, accountability, progress monitoring and engagement.

In this book, we have shown how complexity and volatility are not only increasing but are also having a more pervasive effect on organisations. We have shown how this complexity and volatility is resulting in more surprising events and disruptions and how these are impeding strategy execution and threatening the future viability of organisations. We have also outlined how recent advances in our understanding of strategy execution and complexity have resulted in a number of strategy execution processes and approaches to understanding complexity being available to organisations. We have shown how ambidexterity can be used to achieve the optimal balance between exploitation of immediate opportunities and exploration of tomorrow's opportunities and threats. We have then identified some essential activities that strategic leaders can carry out to maximise the execution effectiveness of their organisations.

Notes

1 Sargut, G., & McGrath, R. (2011). Learning to live with complexity. *Harvard Business Review, 89*(9), 68.

2 Kotter, J. (2011). Can you handle an exponential rate of change? *Forbes,* July.

3 Burgelman, R. A. (1991). Intraorganizational ecology of strategy making and organizational adaptation: Theory and field research. *Organization Science, 2*(3), 239–262.

4 Sydow, J., Schreyögg, G., & Koch, J. (2009). Organizational path dependence: Opening the black box. *Academy of Management Review, 34*(4), 689–709.

5 Burgelman, R. A. (1991). Intraorganizational ecology of strategy making and organizational adaptation: Theory and field research. *Organization Science, 2*(3), 239–262.

6 Gerstner Jr, L. V. (2009). *Who says elephants can't dance?: Leading a great enterprise through dramatic change.* Grand Rapids, MI: Zondervan.

7 Hardy, Q. (2015). Meg Whitman seeks reinvention for HP as it prepares for split, *The New York Times,* October 30.

8 Burgelman, R. A. (1991). Intraorganizational ecology of strategy making and organizational adaptation: Theory and field research. *Organization Science, 2*(3), 239–262.

9 Burgelman, R. A. (1991). Intraorganizational ecology of strategy making and organizational adaptation: Theory and field research. *Organization Science, 2*(3), 239–262.

10 Burgelman, R. A., & Grove, A. S. (2007). Let chaos reign, then rein in chaos – repeatedly: Managing strategic dynamics for corporate longevity. *Strategic Management Journal, 28*(10), 964–979.

11 Raisch, S., Birkinshaw, J., Probst, G., & Tushman, M. L. (2009). Organizational ambidexterity: Balancing exploitation and exploration for sustained performance. *Organization Science, 20,* 685–695.

12 Gibson, C. B., & Birkinshaw, J. (2004). The antecedents, consequences, and mediating role of organizational Ambidexterity. *Academy of Management Journal, 47*(2), 209–226.

13 He, Z., & Wong, P.-K. (2004). Exploration vs. exploitation: An empirical test of the ambidexterity hypothesis. *Organization Science, 15*(4), 481–494.

14 Gibson, C. B., Birkinshaw, J. (2004). The antecedents, consequences, and mediating role of organizational Ambidexterity. *Academy of Management Journal, 47*(2), 209–226.

15 O'Reilly III, C. A., & Tushman, M. L. (2004). The ambidextrous organization. *Harvard Business Review, 82*(4), 74.

16 O'Reilly III, C. A., & Tushman, M. L. (2013). Organizational ambidexterity: Past, present, and future. *Academy of Management Perspectives, 27*(4), 324–338.

17 Tushman, M. L., Smith, W. K., & Binns, A. (2011). The ambidextrous CEO. *Harvard Business Review, 89*(6), 74–80.

18 Govindarajan, V., & Srinivas, S. (2013). The innovation mindset in action: 3M corporation. *Harvard Business Review,* August.

19 Govindarajan, V., & Srinivas, S. (2013). The innovation mindset in action: 3M corporation. *Harvard Business Review,* August.

20 Reeves, M., Love, C., & Tillmans, P. (2012). Your strategy needs a strategy. *Harvard Business Review, 90*(9), 76.
21 Davis, J., Eisenhardt, K. M., & Bingham, C. B. (2009). Optimal structure, market dynamism, and the strategy of simple rules. *Administrative Science Quarterly, 54*, 413–452.
22 Raisch, S., Birkinshaw, J., Probst, G., & Tushman, M. L. (2009). Organizational ambidexterity: Balancing exploitation and exploration for sustained performance. *Organization Science, 20*, 685–695.
23 Burgelman, R. A., & Grove, A. S. (2007). Let chaos reign, then rein in chaos – repeatedly: Managing strategic dynamics for corporate longevity. *Strategic Management Journal, 28*(10), 964–979.
24 Busulwa, R. (2016). The relationship between strategy execution and complexity (PhD Thesis). University of South Australia, Adelaide, SA.
25 Busulwa, R. (2016). The relationship between strategy execution and complexity (PhD Thesis). University of South Australia, Adelaide, SA.
26 Hakimi, S. (2015). Why purpose-driven companies are often more successful, *Fast Company*, July.

Index